# Thirty Days
## *to* Better
## Board Members
## *and*
# Meetings

Church Board Governance and Leadership
Tips That Have a Positive Impact

Jerry W. Storz

WESTBOW
PRESS®
A DIVISION OF THOMAS NELSON
& ZONDERVAN

WestBow Press books may be ordered through booksellers or by contacting:

WestBow Press
A Division of Thomas Nelson & Zondervan
1663 Liberty Drive
Bloomington, IN 47403
www.westbowpress.com
844-714-3454

ISBN: 978-1-6642-8419-7 (sc)
ISBN: 978-1-6642-8420-3 (hc)
ISBN: 978-1-6642-8421-0 (e)

Library of Congress Control Number: 2022921700

Print information available on the last page.

WestBow Press rev. date: 12/8/2022

There are people who come into your life by birth and sometimes by God's providential guidance. Who knew that more than fifty years ago, as I watched my dad, Charles Lewis Storz, serve as a board member in a small church in St. Louis, Missouri, his service would influence and impact my interests in board members' motivation and contribution to serving? I witnessed my dad experience board member service: the good, bad, and ugly. It was through his service that he would often remind our family, "When people disappoint, this is when we keep our eyes on Jesus." Thanks, Dad, for the advice. It has served me well through the years as I have responded to the call to ministry to serve Christ and His church.

My mother-in-law, Rose Mary Niehaus, was another board member I had the privilege to observe. Her love for the church and its impact on the community were her watchword and song! She served the church well as a board member, Sunday school teacher, and church pianist. Thanks, Rose Mary, for showing your favorite son-in-law (your only son-in-law) what it means to love God and serve His church.

A few years back, as I was perusing my college magazine, I noticed they were recognizing one of the alumni, Kent Stroman, who had just written a book entitled *The Intentional Accidental Board*. I immediately did an Amazon search, found the book, and was so excited that "one of my own" had the same passion that I did about board governance and had even written a book about the topic! On a whim, I emailed him and introduced myself, thinking, *What are the chances that an accomplished author like Kent Stroman is going to respond to me?* It was just a day or two later, I received an email response from Kent, and it was like we have been friends forever!

Kent has been such an encourager as we have had discussions about this writing project, all things boards (good, bad, and ugly), and I have become a fan and follower of Kent Stroman. He knows his stuff and shares his knowledge of board governance and fundraising through webinars, writing, workshops, email, and even phone calls. Thanks, Kent, for responding to my email (I hope you are not regretting that response), for your influence, and most importantly, for your friendship.

# contents

# *acknowledgments*

I wish I had paid closer attention in my high school and college English writing classes. As found in *The Van Nuys News* (1949), "Most people's hindsight is 20/20." Perhaps by doing so, the process of writing would have been a little bit easier, grammar rules would have been followed, and spell-check would not have bogged down.

To have an opportunity to fulfill this bucket list item of writing a book seems unreal. My high school English teacher, Mr. Gacksetter, and my college English professor, Mary Ann Galloway, would be so pleasantly surprised to see this book written with my name as the author! To have an opportunity to take a topic that I am passionate about, add to the discussion, and the topic seems unreal.

I want to thank my wife, Delberta Niehaus Storz, who has always encouraged, believed, and expressed her love and support in the adventures, dreams, and goals I have pursued to help me become the person I am today.

This book would not be a reality without the editorial assistance and continuous proofing of Judith Ann Ballou and Augusta Sue Washburn. These ladies have served as my coaches, mentors, and friends. Their patience and encouragement have helped this writing project become a reality.

I cannot acknowledge everyone who has contributed to my interests and passion for faith-based board governance. I sincerely thank all the board members who have added to my knowledge, piqued my interest, and influenced me to attempt this task. There are board members from days spent in Kansas, Missouri, Texas, and Colorado who have contributed to this book you are now holding in your hand.

In closing, I have to say thanks to my colleagues at Nazarene Bible

College who extended a sabbatical for me to embark and complete this book writing project. May the Lord continue to bless Nazarene Bible College as we fulfill our mission to "prepare adults to evangelize, disciple, and minister to the world."

# how to use this book

This is not one of those books that I would suggest you sit down in one sitting and read from cover to cover. Though it can be done, it just would not be the purpose of the book. The book was written so you as an individual who has been asked to serve on a faith-based board, for the individual who has been serving, and for the current board to use as a devotional and discussion guide. It also could be used at the annual board retreat or the board orientation meetings. The purpose of the book is to read it, digest it, and discuss it with your board member peers. Our prayer is that after you have read it, digested it, and applied the board principles or best practices, you will see there is a purpose in your board member service.

You will notice that in the design of the book, a board governance principle or best practice is introduced and discussed. Then the "Pause and Reflect" section of the book ties in a scriptural thought and devotional that aligns with the board principle. A "Think It Through" section follows, asking readers a series of questions to help them apply the board governance principle discovered in the chapter with space to write a response. Taking the time to write a response creates a higher percentage that what was read or discovered will have a greater likelihood of being remembered, than if you just asked a reader to give a "read and reflect" response. The closing section is a prayer that reiterates the board governance principle and recognizes a board member service is indeed a spiritual act of worship. My prayer is that you will see that serving as a board member can and is an enjoyable experience.

# *introduction*

My passion for board service and all things board governance goes back to my elementary school days. I watched my parents serve as church board members and hold ministry positions in a small church with all the highs and lows and joys and struggles that came with their service. Sadly to say, I watched my parents become disillusioned with the church and walk away from their trust of people in ministry (both laity and clergy) and choose never to actively pursue engagement in service to the local church from those days forward.

Fast-forward with me as I entered church staff ministry, fresh out of college, and had the opportunity to work with, watch, and engage with board members in that role. I worked with board members who understood their purposes, roles, and responsibilities in serving. Then I watched board members who used their roles for power, prestige, and an opportunity to pursue their own agendas.

After college, my career took me into the faith-based nonprofit sector, and once again I found myself engaged with organizations governed by board members on both sides of the spectrum. Some knew their roles and responsibilities, and others clearly did not understand. In those years of observing and watching boards of churches and faith-based organizations struggle, I found myself asking, "Where is the disconnect?" How have there been so many churches and faith-based organizations that have been governed by volunteer board members where the confusion, politics, personal agendas, and lack of clarity have kept them from contributing successfully or perhaps even benefiting themselves from their board member service?

After extensive research utilizing a case-study approach to answer this never-ending question, I earned my doctorate in organizational leadership. Board governance was a huge part of that study. Successful faith-based board governance and service are not so much knowing the roles and responsibilities but knowing the One who has called you to serve. Is this your spiritual act of worship?

Through studying faith-based board members' behavior, I want to offer nuggets of truth from both scripture and board governance tips I have gathered over these last few years and bring the two together. Other authors have looked at the relationship between spirituality and board governance. One tool that helped many board members is to engage in a vibrant prayer ministry and devotional reading. The two go hand in hand, like peanut butter and jelly, Batman and Robin, mac and cheese, Bert and Ernie, and Sonny and Cher. I think you get the idea!

My prayer is that as a result of this work, board members will grow in their spiritual lives and grow in their board knowledge. My hope is that board members will come to know what it means to serve joyfully and contribute successfully to the organizations they have agreed to serve.

One will notice that throughout this book, there are numerous sources referenced. As a Christian educator who is called to equip the saints (Ephesians 4), I cannot help but include in this book sources that will add to the knowledge of all things board for those who are currently serving as board members and for those yet to serve. I do not apologize for including these and realize that most individuals picking up a book on board service would be surprised to find such numerous references and sources. May these encourage you to dive in deeper to a greater study and understanding of what it means to serve with excellence.

# *chapter one*

## How Do Board Members Contribute to the Success of the Organizations They Serve?

Y ou have been asked, nominated, elected, or appointed to serve on the board of your local church or a faith-based organization. You are honored that you have been asked. As you process the invitation, you begin to think about the organization. *Why do they want me to serve? Is it because of my expertise? Is it because of my education? Is it because of my involvement? Is it because of my financial investment? Why?* All of those are good reasons that an organization would want you to serve as a board member. Reality says for you to think about the spiritual depth or leadership you can bring to the organization. Perhaps it is in serving this organization that your faith journey begins to deepen. Serving in the board member role will allow you to serve and lead like Jesus. It just may be that for a time like this, God would have you serve as a board member to worship Him as you serve and contribute to the organization's success.

When board members are in a board meeting, they are board members. When they are outside the boardroom, they are volunteers of the organization. Here's the caveat though. As the organization grows and staff is added, it is imperative that the board steps away from being a working board with multifaceted roles and allows the staff to take on its assigned tasks and responsibilities. Staff reports to the senior pastor or executive director and never to the board.

If the premise we are proposing is that serving on a faith-based board is or should be viewed as an opportunity to serve the Lord, then this is the time for you to thank the Lord for the opportunity to serve. Thank Him for the gifts He has given you to serve the church or ministry. Do not take the invitation to serve in this board position lightly. Realize that as you serve, in reality, you are engaged in serving and worshipping the God who has called you for such a time as this.

Your greatest fear about serving is that you may not feel qualified; have the expertise or knowledge; or know the who, what, when, why, or how to amend, second, or discuss an action item or what is meant by *Robert's Rules of Order* or when Robert was elected to the board. It is not often board members are born with the board skills, abilities, and knowledge. Every board member brings his or her experiences, knowledge (albeit limited), and willingness to learn and be trained and grow in boardmanship skills and abilities. It begins with an open and willing heart to learn, serve, and grow.

Effective board governance in church or faith-based organizations utilizes a self-evaluation process. The annual process consists of a checklist that allows the board to identify its roles and responsibilities that are seen to be crucial in leading the organization. Remember only you can answer the question of why you agreed to serve as a board member. Could the reasons be to give back, to learn, to have fun, or to take your turn to serve?

# *Pause and Reflect*

Take a moment to reflect on what scripture has to say about serving as a board member. Space has been created for you to write your responses to the questions asked in this section.

## You Are Serving the Lord Christ

> Whatever you do, work at it with all your heart, as working for the Lord, not for human masters, since you know that you will receive an inheritance from the Lord as a reward. It is the Lord Christ you are serving. (Colossians 3:23–24 NIV)

Paul reminded the believers in Colossae that living as servant leaders would be modeling their lives after the One often referred to as the Suffering Servant. Throughout scripture, we find who Jesus is and the model and message He set for all; Jesus came to serve rather than to be served. "Christian believers must serve others to follow Christ" (The Disciple's Study Bible, 2017). Whether you were elected, selected, asked, nominated, or sought out to serve as a board member, remember the bottom line is you are serving Christ in this role. As a faith-based board member, have you ever thought of your board service as serving the Lord Christ? Perhaps a better way of asking or thinking about your service as a board member is in a series of questions.

# *Think It Through*

1. Why are you serving?

2. What is your motivation to serve?

3. How is your service contributing to the success of the organization?

# *Prayer*

Father, thanks for giving me this opportunity to serve as a board member. I do not take this opportunity lightly. I pray that as I serve in my board member role, You will be pleased with my service. Let my service reflect the prayer of the psalmist.

May the words of my mouth and the meditation of my heart be pleasing to you, O Lord, my rock and my redeemer. (Psalm 19:14 NLT)

# chapter two

## Governance

L et us spend the next few chapters discussing all things board. The first thing we're going to address is this thing called governance. What do we mean by governance?

Governance is more than hiring, firing, evaluating, and setting the compensation for the senior pastor or executive director. Governance is about reviewing the strategic plans, overseeing the budget, and reviewing the financial statements. Keep in mind that board members have both legally mandated governance functions and other duties. Governance is the legal, moral, and ethical responsibility of the board. This is why it is important for a board member to attend board meetings. Governance happens at board meetings. Board governance consists of many pieces. These include board structure and processes, strategic planning, and assigning duties and responsibilities. Evaluation of

> *Governance is the process and procedures in which organizations direct and manage themselves to reduce risks.*

programs is always the key to success. Boards should be taking a more active role in the required reporting that the IRS requires from the 990 forms for nonprofit organizations(https://efile.form990.org).

This form now asks numerous questions about board structures, practices, and policies. It is designed to illuminate the inner workings of organizations and ask questions that focus on how faith-based boards perform their roles and responsibilities.

There are several strategies that could be employed as an organization looks at the governance duties of board members. One approach would be to designate half the board as having governance functions and responsibilities. The other half would not be required to have governance functions or responsibilities. These individuals could serve on other designated board committees. It is important to not make those who choose not to serve as governance board members second-class citizens or to be viewed as insignificant board members. It is a process of allowing and helping board members to serve in roles that speak to their expertise, interests, and passion.

Some churches allow their boards to divide themselves into stewards, trustees, and educational committees. Each of these committees has distinct responsibilities to ensure the care of the church members, property, and its influence and impact on the community.

Other organizations utilize a board governance committee to ensure the board is fulfilling its duties and responsibilities. Its responsibilities are to review the governance structure (appendix A) and practices of the organization and report its findings and recommendations to the board.

Whatever approach or strategy by which an organization chooses to govern itself, the challenge is to never settle. Always strive for the best and to be the best.

# Pause and Reflect

Take a moment to reflect on what scripture has to say about serving as a board member. Space has been created for you to write your responses to the questions asked in this section.

## Entrusted with Much

> From everyone who has been given much, much will be demanded; and from the one who has been entrusted with much, much more will be asked. (Luke 12:48 NIV)

You thought serving as a board member would require you to show up for a once-a-month meeting, hear reports from the executive director or staff, review the financial report, and approve next year's budget, and you would be done within an hour, right? Wrong. Who are we kidding? Have you been surprised by all the things you are doing that they did not tell you you would be doing when you agreed to serve on the board? Maybe they did prepare you for your service by taking you through a time of orientation, reviewing the history of the organization, and identifying the strengths, weaknesses, opportunities, and threats of the organization. Perhaps you were even presented with a board member notebook with the last three months of board business, reports, and financials. However you landed in the board seat you are now occupying, you are either responding with "I'm so glad I said yes to this opportunity" or "Stop this ride. I want to get off!"

My prayer for you as you serve in your board member role is that you realize that much is required of you. The old adage "With great power comes great responsibility" rings true for those who agree to serve as board members. Others are depending on you to give direction and instill purpose and guidance for the success and future of the organization.

# Think It Through

1.  What has God uniquely given the church or organization regarding finances, resources, staffing, etc.?

2.  How should the board use what God has given the church or organization?

3.  How can you serve God in your board member role and responsibilities?

# *Prayer*

Father, as I reflect on all that You have given the church or organization in which I am serving as a board member, first I want to thank You. Second, I want to make sure that I am being a good steward of all that You have given us. I do not want to take the finances, resources, staff, or volunteers for granted. Help me serve You as I serve in this role.

# *chapter three*

## Fiduciary Duties

L et me introduce another board governance term that may be new to you. You may stumble and stammer like I do as you say it. Say it with me, "Fiduciary duties." Say it ten times in a row! How did you do? "What in the world does this word even mean?" you may be asking. I am glad you are asking, seeking clarification, and growing in your board knowledge and understanding.

*Fiduciary* means board members are serving and fulfilling their roles in an objective, unselfish, responsible, honest, trustworthy, and efficient manner. In serving, it is not about them; they do not benefit from their service as board members. In fulfilling your fiduciary duties, you are in essence asking thoughtful questions and challenging problematic situations.

In fulfilling their fiduciary responsibilities, board members are treating the organization's assets and resources with the same care they would treat their own resources.

Best practices are that a board gives oversight to the finances of the organization. This really goes beyond a best practice; it is a general expectation of board members to understand and embrace fiduciary responsibilities. To successfully fulfill this duty requires board members to read and understand the organization's financial statements. This task in itself has to be a collaborative effort among the senior pastor and staff that enables the board to fulfill its fiduciary responsibilities by presenting a financial plan that is fiscally responsible.

The senior pastor and staff must take careful attention and consideration to operate and respect the operating budget with a sound and prudent mindset.

Lack of training and development has contributed to board members and churches that have minimal or limited fiduciary knowledge. In order to see a change in this scenario, organizations and their leaders must commit to board member development, and board members must commit the time needed to understand and fulfill their fiduciary responsibilities. The following questions need to be addressed by potential board members before joining a board:

- Is the financial condition of the organization sound?
- Does the board discuss and approve the annual budget?
- How often do board members receive financial reports?
- Can you see the organization's three most recent Form 990s? (These are tax returns for nonprofit, tax-exempt organizations.)

Again, reiterating the fiduciary responsibilities lie with board members. Though an organization may elect to have various committees to help guide the work of the board (e.g., board training, orientation, education, finance, and governance), the fiduciary responsibilities and board governance still remain the responsibility of the elected board.

One does not have to look too hard to find reports of nonprofit organization boards that have failed in fulfilling their fiduciary duties. Sad to say, this has proven to be true for churches and faith-based boards as well.

As a board member, there are duties and legal responsibilities you must be aware of that are often referred to as the "the D's of good governance."

## DUTY OF CARE

This means board members should fulfill their roles to the best of their abilities by proactively participating and communicating. It is suggested that board members should be reasonably informed about the organization's activities, participate in decisions, and do so in good faith.

## DUTY OF LOYALTY

All activities should be done in the best interests of the organization, not in the best interests of individual board members. A board member should remain faithful and loyal to the organization and avoid conflicts of interest. If a board member cannot in good conscience avoid conflicts or sign the conflict-of-interest document, then such board member has the responsibility to remove themselves from any board action item that would be considered or misconstrued as a conflict of interest.

## DUTY OF OBEDIENCE

The board should follow organizational rules as defined in the governance documents. A board member should focus on the central purposes of the organization and respect all laws and legal regulations.

## DUTY OF KNOWLEDGE

The informed board member is aware and has knowledge of the direction in which the organization is headed and if the organization is fulfilling its purpose. As the board is allowed to ask questions, seek clarification, and meet the expectations of their service, then when the organization faces challenges or strategizes for its future, board members can be assured it remains on track. The axiom "Ignorance of the law is no excuse" means you cannot defend your actions by arguing you did not know they were illegal, even if you honestly did not realize you were breaking the law. How often do faith-based board members try to live by this same principle when it comes to governance? It is expected that board members have the knowledge and are aware of their roles and responsibilities and what it means to govern and contribute to the success of the organization. As a board member, can you answer the following knowledge questions?

- What are the mission, vision, and values?
- Why does the organization exist?
- Whom does it serve?
- What is the plan to fulfill its mandate?
- What are the results?
- To whom is the organization accountable?
- What is the act under which the organization was incorporated?
- What are other laws that may affect the organization?
- What are the bylaws of the organization?
- What are the applicable codes or regulations?
- Is there a policy manual?

## CONFLICT-OF-INTEREST POLICY

This is a situation in which the personal or professional concerns of a member of the board or staff may affect his or her ability to put the welfare of the organization before the benefit of himself or another party. This policy needs to be a part of the board members' orientation and training and reviewed annually.

Board members' fiduciary responsibilities ensure the fulfillment of the organization's mission and the legal accountability of all operations. Board members have a responsibility for financial viability and proper handling of financial matters.

Please do not let the term *fiduciary* scare you away and keep you from serving. Understand that it means more than reading the financial statements or a treasurer's report.

Your role as a board member is to lead, not to follow others, and vote as they vote or to become the yes person on the board. To lead means to ask questions clarifying questions. A healthy board allows questions to be asked. This helps you understand everything that is at stake and being considered or not being considered.

In fulfilling fiduciary duties, board members are recognizing the good that is being done (mission is being met). There will be opportunities to lead, ask questions, and address problematic situations. Did you catch that one little word in the above? Actually, it is not a little word. It is a huge word for board members to note. The word is *lead!* Leading comes from being engaged and not neglecting the responsibilities of ensuring the church or organization is reaching its potential and meeting the mission. *To lead* means to become more than a passive or present board member. Strive to become an exceptional board member.

# Pause and Reflect

Take a moment to reflect on what scripture has to say about serving as a board member. Space has been created for you to write your responses to the questions asked in this section.

## The Parable of the Talents

A man going on a journey gives portions of his estate
to three servants, who each make choices …
—Matthew 25:14–30 (NIV)

As one reads the parable of the talents, how does this story resonate with you? Do you see any correlation between using your gifts, talents, and abilities to doing the work God has called you to do as a board member? Do you see this parable as servants who wasted the master's money or as an opportunity of being good stewards?

# *Think It Through*

1. What information and/or education do board members need in order to understand and respond more effectively to the financial situation of the organization?

2. As a board member, did you experience board orientation? If you did, what was included in the orientation? If you did not, what reasons were you given for not having an orientation? If you did experience an orientation, who was involved in the orientation? When did the orientation take place? Did the orientation help prepare you as you stepped into your board member role? What was the strength or weakness of the orientation?

# *Prayer*

Lord, thank You for the opportunity to use my gifts and talents as a board member. Help me not to take my responsibilities lightly or to waste the opportunities You have given me. Help me to know and understand the responsibilities I have to contribute to the success of the organizations in which I serve.

# chapter four

## Mission

Hollywood introduced the adage "You had one job to do" in a well-known Las Vegas casino heist movie. The earliest known mention of the phrase can be heard when a character scolds his team for missing a step that singlehandedly leads to the failure of an otherwise well-planned vault heist.

When it comes to board service, the board has one overarching job: ensuring there is a mission strategy in place and working beside the senior pastor or executive director to achieve that mission. Most faith communities develop a mission statement. The board of directors is charged with ensuring that the organization stays true to its mission and operates in compliance with its established policies.

Board members carry the responsibility for keeping focus on the organizational mission. What keeps boards from doing this one job? Do board members understand the organization's values, mission, and vision? Can board members recite the mission? When board members know and can articulate the mission, they can monitor and offer resources so the organization has informed members versus uninformed or unengaged members.

Careful consideration must be given to how reports and the information within the reports are communicated to the board. Awareness of biases from both the persons preparing and presenting the reports have to be taken into consideration. In addition, board members need to be aware of the potential biases and how these may have influenced the preparer and preparation of the reports. Healthy organizations have a regular and structured process whereby information is shared, concerns are addressed in a safe and trustworthy environment, and challenges and problems are resolved.

The board is responsible to ensure that the organization is achieving its mission effectively and efficiently. In order to fulfill this responsibility, it is imperative that the board receives reliable and valid information on the health and how things are going for the organization.

There are metrics that churches and faith-based organizations can use to determine their missional health. Churches measure success in the number of conversions, baptisms, or new members. Another metric might include the number of small groups or discipleship ministries started or experiencing growth both numerically and spiritually (manifestation of the gifts or fruits of the Spirit in small-group members' lives) or an increase in finances (stewardship) or the overall financial health of the organization.

In faith-based organizations, the measurement of success or impact is not based on the charisma, passion, and vision of the leader. There needs to be a balance between anecdotal and evidence-based support for the measurement of the success and impact of faith-based organizations.

Keep this thought in mind as you are defining or measuring success in both the church and faith-based world. Success is measured by the social and spiritual impact on its intended communities. There is nothing unspiritual about measuring and communicating the impact organizations are having. Measuring and communicating impact allow successes to be celebrated.

There are countless stories told of churches, faith-based organizations, higher education institutions, and for-profit organizations that have experienced mission drift. Mission drift happens when inadequate attention is given to details, such as job descriptions, program outlines, and event plans.

A church plans for its future, exercises good stewardship, and creates innovative programming to make a difference in its community and or world.

The question becomes this: why and how do some boards miss the mark and what to do? Fram (2022) has identified four areas where boards are coming up short in their performance.

1.  **Knowledge Gaps:** Many new board members are in the dark about some of the operating issues facing their organizations.
    **Solution**: Provide a time of orientation. "Orientations can take a variety of forms, ranging from brief preboard sessions to premeeting phone calls from the CEO or board chair. These updates will provide the new board member with information that should make his/her participation in the board meeting more meaningful."

2.  **Lack of Self-Assessment**: When it comes to the (business) boards assessing their own performance, this is often done by using the check-in-the-box exercise (along) with some form of gentle peer review, reports Miles. In the nonprofit environment, board self-assessments are not usually a priority because nonprofit directors often have time constraints.
    **Solution**: Boards need to make good faith efforts to have reasonable self-reviews. Keep in mind that board members may hesitate to negatively reflect that fellow board members have been poor decision-makers.

3.  **Self-Delusion:** "Management capture" occurs when a board too readily accepts a delusional view from management that organizational performance is significantly better than reality.
    **Solution**: Boards should develop rigorous impact measures, both quantitative and qualitative, by which to judge organizational and board performance. Models for self-board assessments are available from professional groups and consultants.

4.  **Recruitment Shortcomings and Board Inexperience:** Board members lack experience in succession planning. The board culture consists of those with limited or no board experience.
    **Solution**: To address the lack of experience challenge, board members need to be active in their roles engaging individually and collectively to add to their board knowledge, whether this is through webinars, seminars, or informal or formal training.

A conscientious pursuit of these goals will enable boards to be "on the mark" and help guide the organization in fulfilling its mission.

As we end our discussion on the mission, we find ourselves circling back to the *governance* term again. All board members should be concerned about governance. This concern about governance leads to what could be best practices. Governance is not about power; it is not about board members meddling in the day-to-day operations. It is about board members knowing and understanding their roles and responsibilities, helping identify, think through, guard, and protect its mission.

# Pause and Reflect

Take a moment to reflect on what scripture has to say about serving as a board member. Space has been created for you to write your responses to the questions asked in this section.

**The Fellowship of the Believers**
They devoted themselves to the apostles' teaching and to
fellowship, to the breaking of bread and to prayer.
—Acts 2:42 (NIV)

A few years ago, I wrote an article for *Entre Nino's Spanish Children's Ministry Magazine* (www.entreninos.com) entitled "The Five Functions." Here's an excerpt from that article:

> Lately, I've been challenged by a church strategy that has been around for a while and some would say was introduced by Rick Warren in his book *The Purpose Driven Church*. However, research indicates that Warren really did not introduce the five functions of the church. In reality, it has been around in some shape and form as long as there have been individuals (educators, consultants, and various experts) talking about church growth strategies. Do not check out just yet. Life has a way of repeating itself, or is that history has a way of repeating itself? I want to use this article as an opportunity to challenge you to think about the functions of not only your church, but as your responsibilities as a board member. I cannot help but think that if we had board members living, implementing, and evaluating their mission and purpose by these five functions, then both the Great Commandment (Matthew 22:37) and Great Commission (Matthew 28:19–20) will be met.

Church growth is the natural result of church health. But church health can only occur when our message is biblical and our mission is balanced. Each of the five New Testament purposes of the church must be in balance with the others for health to occur.

# Think It Through

As you think about your ministry or your church or organization:

1. How is your church measuring up in these five functions? What is missing? What could be improved on? Which of these functions has the highest priority? Who is the driving force behind these functions, and how they are carried out?

2. What is the purpose (mission) of the ministry? Is it meeting the needs of the community? What would happen to the ministry if you stepped down from serving as a board member? What would happen if the ministry closed its doors? Would anyone in the community notice?

# *Prayer*

Father, the church has been gathering for quite a long time. It has gathered for fellowship, breaking of bread, singing hymns, and offering up prayers of thanks and supplications to You and will continue to do so, until Your return. You have given us one another to encourage, share, and love. Help us to take care of each other. To reach out to people who need to experience love, acceptance, and forgiveness. Help us not to be consumed with being right but just getting it right. Help us to be good stewards of the body and fellowship of the believers.

# chapter five

## Vision

I desperately want to depart from the duties of governance and what it means to be an effective board member. But at each turn and section, it seems I cannot get away from this idea. So if you will indulge me for just one more dive into this duty conversation, I will do my best to move on to the fun stuff—no promises, but I will do my best to move on! And yes, there can be fun and positive experiences from serving on a board!

The first order of business we need to address is this: what is a vision statement? Vision statements look to the future and what we would like to see and be. A formal vision statement usually contains the values and beliefs that guide the organization. The crafting of the vision statement is not one individual's assignment or task. It is a group process; it is allowing each and every board member to share his or her perspective on what the organization is about and what it is working toward.

To get in a frame of mind of thinking about the future, we have to ask a few strategic-planning-type questions. One question that might provide focus is this: what words would you like to see being used to describe the church, ministry, or organization in the future? Asking this type of question moves individuals from what the organization looks like now or the problems that they perceive, or why they think things can never change.

Do not allow the word *vision* to become a buzzword and lose its meaning and significance for your church or ministry. Become the ministry that knows where it is headed and how it is going to get there. As a leader, you will have an opportunity to visit, revisit, and recast the vision statement as the ministry experiences growth and changes. Continue to seek God's direction and will for your work.

# *Pause and Reflect*

Take a moment to reflect on what scripture has to say about serving as a board member. Space has been created for you to write your responses to the questions asked in this section.

## Seek Me and Find Me

You will seek me and find me when
you seek me with all your heart.
—Jeremiah 29:13 (NIV)

What would happen as you serve if you began to live out the instructions found in the passage from Jeremiah? Jesus reminds us in Matthew 6:33 (NIV), "But seek first the kingdom of God and his righteousness, and all these things will be added to you." It certainly appears that Jesus was emphasizing the importance of seeking the wisdom and guidance of Him in our lives as we make decisions and seek direction, purpose, and meaning. We live in a broken world. We live in a world of people who are seeking answers, hope, and solutions to all that has been thrown their way. Even faith-based organizations face uncertain times. Conflicts are not new to the faith-based world. May I remind you of the struggles of the early church? The good news is that the early church and its leaders never lost sight of their vision to reach any and all with the life-changing message of Christ!

# *Think It Through*

1. As a board member, can you describe the mission, vision, and goals of the organization?

2. Give a thumbnail sketch of the organizational structure and overall financial situation.

3. Provide information about programs and services provided.

4. Can you articulate your personal commitment to the organization and reasons for joining the board?

5. Do the board and senior pastor or executive director have a collective vision of how the organization should be evolving over the next three to five years?

## Prayer

Father, thank You for the opportunity You have given to me as a board member to speak about the vision of the ministry. Let me always seek You first as I lead, evaluate, and offer wisdom and insight as a board member.

# chapter six

## Values

D o you know the values of the organization in which you serve? Do your own values align with the organization? If I were to ask you to write your values, could you write down at least your top five? If I were to ask you the top five values of the organization, could you identify them? Take some time and think through some major events that have happened in the life of the organization. Think about the wins and losses. Values may shift over time. The organization needs to take the time to identify and clarify its values often. This will save lots of headaches later.

Every organization or church has a history. Tradition, theological roots, and spiritual values encompass each of these. Board members should know and celebrate these.

There is a myriad of reasons why people join boards. One of the reasons is they enjoy collaborating with interesting people who have the same interests and values as they do.

As you have discovered or will soon discover, serving as a board member is one of the most challenging and rewarding volunteer assignments. Do yourself a service; ask questions before agreeing to serve. See if your values align with the church. Are there policies in place that articulate the values and define scopes of authority and limitations, guidelines, and boundaries to be observed by staff, board members, and committees? What is your motivation for serving? Is serving on this board a good fit with your skills, abilities, and interests? Has the organization taken the time to develop the board into a cohesive team with shared values?

# Pause and Reflect

Take a moment to reflect on what scripture has to say about serving as a board member. Space has been created for you to write your responses to the questions asked in this section.

## The Cost of Being a Disciple

> Which of you, wishing to build a tower, does not first sit down and count the cost to see if he has the resources to complete it?
> —Luke 14:28 (NIV)

With the mind and spirit of Christ as its integrating center, the Christ-centered organization is a dynamic movement toward wholeness.

- All of its members are personally committed to Jesus Christ and to the outworking of the Great Commission in the purpose of the organization.
- All of its members find meaning in their lives and satisfaction in their work by being a partner in the ministry with all other members.
- All of its members are motivated by the redemptive hope of seeing God's will done in the contemporary world and anticipating His coming in glory.

# *Think It Through*

1. How do board members become aware of the organization's mission, history, and values?

2. How are key groups, such as staff and stakeholders, taught the organization's theological heritage and defining characteristics? In what ways do a shared commitment to the organization's story and values shape strategic decisions?

3. What are the core values of the organization? What does the organization do? For whom does the organization do what it does? What demonstrable benefits do stakeholders of the organization receive from their experience with the organization?

# *Prayer*

Father, I want to value what You value. As I read Your Word, I see that You value life. You came to give us life and to give us life more abundantly. I know You valued love because You demonstrated the greatest way to show love by giving Your life so I can live forever with You. I know You value peace. I can have peace through You. I know You valued truth. You are the truth, You define truth, and it is through Your truth we have life. You value knowledge and wisdom. Luke 2:52 states You grew in wisdom and stature and in favor with God and man. And I am to pursue these same traits as I live with others in this fallen world. I can see You value relationships. You spent time with people. You enjoyed people. You chose twelve to carry out the work of Your Father. You have chosen me to do Your will. You have always used people to accomplish Your work. May You be pleased with my work and service as I serve as a board member.

# chapter seven

## Identity

A couple of years ago, my wife and I started watching some land being developed close to our neighborhood. We did not see any signs of what it was going to be. Like most, we were very curious about what was being built. We would drive by and watch the progress. We looked for signs. No signs. We guessed, along with all of our neighbors. We watched our emails and any communication coming from our Nextdoor neighbor app. Spring construction led to summer construction led to fall construction. The building began to take shape. It was a building with no windows and had security fencing around it. There went our thoughts of a new grocery store or retail with a cool coffee shop! A parking lot was created, but no signage of what it was! It drove the community insane!

Then one day news broke that it was a data center. That news only created more questions. A data center for whom? Whom are they collecting data from? How are they getting the data? We have discovered this strange new building in our backyard, a building of the unknown. We drive by it as we go to the nearest grocery store. No name. We see cars. The questions still lurk in the back of our minds on the who, what, where, why, and how of data.

You are probably asking yourself, "What does this have to do with organizational identity?" As a board member, if you are not aware of the organization's identity, reputation, mission, and effectiveness, then the question becomes this: does your church or organization matter? The often quoted, but not quite accurate, quote from Lewis Carroll's classic tale *Alice in Wonderland* states, "If you don't know where you're going, any road will take you there." Identity is key. Members and leaders have to know where the organization is headed. There has to be intentional planning. Leaders must look for opportunities and seek excellence at the forefront. Organizations should exist for a reason. What's yours?

As a board member, keep in mind that you are the group's ambassador, advocate, and community representative. Function as stewards and fulfill your fiduciary responsibilities. The church has a reputation among its stakeholders and in the community. This reputation can either be positive or negative. It can be warranted or unwarranted. As a board member, your responsibility is to be aware of the reputation and the perception both inside and outside the church.

You are responsible for the organization's effectiveness. This is measured by different means. These means may include financial results, conversions, baptisms, education and discipleship ministries, and ministry programming. With the evolution of various social media platforms becoming readily available, news (positive and negative) about the organization can spread pretty quickly. I often tell my students who struggle with online classes for their education, "You can either fight it or embrace it." The same can be said about social media platforms. You must embrace, adapt, and adopt its positive use for your church or become irrelevant. When members experience something new, different, and positive—or negative—these individuals seek various social media platforms to express their likes, dislikes, and experiences. Board members should not shy away from social media communication.

In conflict management, we learn that the issue is not always the issue. As board members, your job is not necessary to wear the referee shirt and grab your whistle. Your job is to listen, respond in love, and love people. Keep this thought in mind as you deal with people who are complainers, negative, gossipers, and naysayers. People who are hurt, hurt other people. Do not become the type of board member who sticks his head in the sand or avoids negative people. Loving people requires seeing beyond their faults to their inner needs and hurts.

How do you view your constituents', stakeholders', and critics' feedback, no matter what form or platform is utilized? Do you value their input and perspective of their experiences? Do you discount their voices and opinions? There are a variety of reasons why people choose or choose not to engage with your organization. Researchers have found that the church has become less a part of American life. How does the leadership respond to this news? Do they discount it or take the time to discover the why? Do they change anything as a result of these findings?

This next thought is probably not covered in too many board orientations, but it should be. Image and identity are not the same. Image is external, and identity is internal. Image refers to how outsiders see your organization. Identity is the values and beliefs that your organization stands for. The board should consistently monitor both.

Faith-based groups that stay connected and tied to events within their community give board members insight into their effectiveness, communication, and influence. Effective boards measure organizational effectiveness and integrity regularly.

# Pause and Reflect

Take a moment to reflect on what scripture has to say about serving as a board member. Space has been created for you to write your responses to the questions asked in this section.

## The Hearing Ear and the Seeing Eye

> The hearing ear, and the seeing eye, the LORD
> hath made even both of them.
> —Proverbs 20:1 (NIV)

What better senses to use in your role and responsibilities as a board member than your ears and eyes? In John 4:35 (NIV) we find, "I tell you, open your eyes and look at the fields! They are ripe for harvest." The time is now to fulfill the mission. It is time to open your eyes, see, and respond to the needs the church was called to fulfill. This is the mission, the mandate, and it can only be met with the board and staff who are focused on its purpose and serving with eyes wide open and ears to hear.

# *Think It Through*

1. If the church closed its doors today, would your stakeholders (members) suffer any real loss?

2. How long would it take, and how difficult would it be, for people to find another church that could meet their needs? As well as you did?

# *Prayer*

Thank You, heavenly Father, for giving me eyes to see, ears to hear, and a voice to speak. Let me use these three senses in my role as a board member not just so my voice or opinions can be heard or recognized. Not just so I can be seen as the board member who is always present and speaks with a voice of authority and finality. But let my voice speak as You would speak. Let my eyes see others as You see them, and let my ears hear the needs of those around me.

# *chapter eigth*

## Governance Models

People often think there is only one governance model for how boards make decisions. According to research, there are eleven different governance models. Did you catch that? Eleven different governance models! Just as a point of information, *Robert's Rules of Order* is not a governance model. *Robert's Rules of Order* is a guide for conducting meetings and making decisions as a group. The board can set a policy by which they want to conduct the business of the board. They can choose to follow *Robert's Rules of Order*, or they can seek other sources to help guide the business of the board. The important thing is that there is an acceptable guide that the board has adopted and follows.

The board model that is best for one organization is not necessarily best for another, and decisions about governance need to be based on the configuration of personalities, culture, and environmental pressures unique to each nonprofit organization. The bylaws often determine how the church is run, business is conducted, and the responsibilities of the board are fulfilled. This is why it is important that the bylaws are reviewed often, if not annually.

Nonprofit boards keep the mission at the forefront when directing the affairs of the organization. Incoming funds are used to support the organization's work. Most board members for nonprofit organizations serve on the board because of their passion and commitment to a cause. While serving on a nonprofit board carries a certain level of honor and prestige, board members need to take an active approach to oversee the organization to prevent problems and legal issues. Nonprofit boards hold responsibility for fiduciary matters as well as matters that have been delegated to others.

The goal in any of the governance models is not to find the perfect model but to establish and implement a governance model that contributes to a healthy organization that is focused on achieving its mission.

There are two basic structures or models for governing boards. These are policy-making boards and administrative boards. Policy-making boards do exactly that—make policies. Those policies are then implemented by the executive director who is hired. Administrative boards play a more active role in managing the operations of the organization along with the staff and various committees. Within these two general categories, there are more specific types of models that can be found at the following web site: https://www.boardeffect.com/blog/board-governance-models-a-comprehensive-list/.

Challenges and rapidly changing environments may make it increasingly difficult for nonprofits to respond to the needs of their community in an effective manner utilizing the traditional governance model, so being open to change is necessary.

In addition to discovering the one best governance model, the argument can easily be made that there is no one best formula or approach for creating effective boards. Sort of like raising kids, perfect world, perfect job, perfect church, board, or perfect anything! May I encourage you to give up the search for the perfect governance model and just land on a governance model that works for your church. In saying this, I'm not giving you permission to dismiss your duties and responsibilities to ensure the meeting of the mission and direction of the church.

As we delve into the policy section of board governance, we have to start by asking, "Does the board function as a policy board or tactical board?" *(Colorado District Church of the Nazarene Pastoral Review,* 2022). As stated earlier, a policy board develops policies, hires and fires the senior pastor or executive director, and requires the leadership of the organization to implement the approved policies. A tactical board would reflect a hands-on or working board—a board that is engaged in the administrative functions of the organization.

Neither governance model is necessarily wrong. It just comes down to the needs of the organization. Keep this thought in mind as you think about the governance model your church or faith-based organization will employ. The policy model is designed to help leaders, board members, and staff to make better collective decisions and guide individual actions and behaviors. Boards and policies need to evolve along with the organization.

If there is a staff that is capable to carry out the strategic plans of the board and organization, then there is no need for a hands-on or working board. In other words, they do not need to plan the color of the napkins for the fall festival or the retirement party for the retiring custodian. When the board gets down in the weeds of planning and doing, then there is a problem. If the board has a policy in place for how to handle the retirement of employees, then its work has been done. The staff is aware of that policy and can carry it out.

Here's the good news about governance: Your church or faith-based organization can have good governance without unnecessary complexity or guilt. How? By applying reasonable and sound policies for oversight of the organization, without having excessive emphasis on board governance models. Boards should be aware of the risks but not forget to focus on the true calling: the effective mission of their organization.

It is recommended that after selecting its governance structure, the board seeks training to understand the model and the roles of the board within that model.

# Pause and Reflect

Take a moment to reflect on what scripture has to say about serving as a board member. Space has been created for you to write your responses to the questions asked in this section.

## Perfect

Be perfect, therefore, as your heavenly Father is perfect.
—Matthew 5:48 (NIV)

I know we stumble over the Bible verse found in Matthew 5:48, "Be perfect, therefore, as your heavenly Father is perfect." And when things do not turn out perfectly, we put ourselves on a guilt trip and wonder why things are not perfect. Remember we live in a fallen world. Yes, God created a perfect world. Then He created man and woman who bought into Satan's lies, and then perfection ended. So man has been toiling and trying to be perfect since that day they bought into Satan's lie and deceit.

Can I encourage you to stop trying to be perfect? Stop trying to create the perfect church, board, or committee, or just stop with the perfection. Just as God took care of the sin problem of Adam and Eve, He knows and can take care of the church with all of its imperfections. He is at work. Take a deep breath, and stop worrying about perfection. Keep this thought from Micah 6:8 (NIV) in mind: "What does the Lord require of you? To act justly, and to love mercy and to walk humbly with your God." Find the balance between inner principles and outward conduct.

# *Think about It*

1. What governance model is your church board or faith-based organization following?

2. What is the best model for the church or organization?

3. Is there room to employ secular governance models with the work of our church or organization (i.e., John Carver's Policy Governance Model for Nonprofits)?

# *Prayer*

Lord, You know what I bring to my board role. You know my strengths and weaknesses better than I do. You know my thoughts before, during, and after a good, bad, or less than exciting board meeting. You know how I evaluate and reflect on what I said or did not say. What others said or did not say. What should have been said, decided on, and tabled. If it sounds like I am worried, stressed, or even frustrated, You are probably right. Remind me it is Your church. You are not looking for perfect people or the perfect church. You are looking for faithful, obedient, and teachable followers.

# chapter nine

## Policies

**H**ang on! We are about to discuss the responsibilities of board members once again. One of them is to be informed about the organization's mission, services, and programs. But your responsibilities also include being aware of the policies, establishing policies, and abiding by such policies.

Does the question become this: who establishes or manages the policies approved by the board? The answer to this is not as complicated as one might think. Are you familiar with the term *self-management*? The board has to manage itself. In other words, it has to make sure it is engaged in good governance. Self-management happens as a board creates structure, policies, and procedures that support good governance.

At this point, we may be asking which areas require policies. We will identify some of these areas. Remember the purpose of policies is not to restrict or hinder your church or ministry from meeting its mission or purpose. The purpose is to protect the staff and board as they facilitate the fulfillment of the mission of the organization.

Some commonly recommended policies include the following:

## CONFLICT-OF-INTEREST POLICY

As a 501(c)(3) nonprofit organization registered with your state and with the nonprofit status, the church and ministry are recognized by the IRS. The IRS requires nonprofit boards to have a conflict-of-interest policy to ensure boards are making decisions objectively. The revised Form 990 asks questions, such as whether the organization has a written conflict-of-interest policy and whether officers, directors, and key employees are required to disclose potential conflicts.

## RECORDS RETENTION AND DESTRUCTION

The 990 forms inquire about the policy in place regarding the church and ministry records and retention. Best practices suggest, at a bare minimum, that a nonprofit should be keeping records for at least three years—or in some cases substantially longer. Such records that should be kept are

- board meeting minutes
- tax documents
- donation records
- records of receipts and disbursements
- contracts

A policy should be established if the records being kept have to be paper or if it is acceptable to be digitized. There also needs to be a policy put in place on how such records can, when, or should be destroyed.

## HUMAN RESOURCE POLICY

This policy helps create and maintain a consistent approach when it comes to determining salaries, wages, and benefits for a nonprofit's employees. If the board creates a separate HR committee to make such decisions, the committee does not have carte blanche but functions as a sanctioned committee of the board. Any recommendations have to be in consideration of the board approved budget (line item) or, if necessary, be approved by the board. Having a policy in place will guide the HR committee in its task.

## FINANCIAL MANAGEMENT POLICY

Having a good financial management policy in place protects the board and staff. It keeps everyone and all monies accountable. It is important to cover details, such as who makes deposits, who has signature authority, and the preapproval requirements.

## VOLUNTEER MANAGEMENT POLICY

Do you know who is the backbone of your ministry or organization? The volunteers! Volunteers are at the heart of a nonprofit. When volunteers are not appreciated or valued, they have a tendency to leave their volunteer positions. Do not assume the volunteers know what is expected of them. Define the expectations for them. Having clear policies and procedures for your volunteers not only sets them up for success but protects the ministry as well. Policy statements clarify rules, regulations, beliefs, and values. Creating a volunteer handbook that outlines policies and procedures for volunteers could serve to clarify expectations, retain volunteers, and ensure the safety of staff, other volunteers, and participants in your ministry. The handbook should include at least the following:

- the ministry's story and mission
- process and procedure for background checks of all staff and volunteers
- volunteer management staffing and contact information

- position descriptions
- emergency procedures
- the ministry statement/policy regarding working with minors and required training

The *Manual* of the Church of the Nazarene states that the business of the local church board shall be

> to adopt and implement a plan to reduce the risk that individuals placed in positions of authority within the church will use the position of trust or authority to engage in misconduct. The plan for each local church must take into consideration its own unique circumstances.

There must be a plan and policy put in place. Again, "policies are what you do, not what you say you do" (nazarenesafe.org/policies).

A board that takes the time to review, question, engage in conversations, and make decisions about its policies is fulfilling its duty.

# Pause and Reflect

Take a moment to reflect on what scripture has to say about serving as a board member. Space has been created for you to write your responses to the questions asked in this section.

## Be a Good Steward

> God's gifts of grace come in many forms. Each of you has received
> a gift in order to serve others. You should use it faithfully. If
> anyone speaks, they should do it as one speaking God's words. If
> anyone serves, they should do it with the strength God provides.
> Then in all things God will be praised through Jesus Christ.
> Glory and power belong to him forever and ever. Amen.
> —1 Peter 4:10–11 (NIRV)

What an honor that as a board member you get to serve others. In your serving, you are not only serving others, but you are ultimately serving God. You are being a good steward of the gifts and graces He has bestowed upon you. In essence, you are allowing yourself to be held responsible and held accountable for His church. You are encouraging others through your service as a board member. You are extending grace where needed. You are giving a helping hand, showing and sharing a caring spirit, giving a gentle response, and reflecting a Savior who loves, accepts, and forgives.

*Think about It*

1. Are your nonprofit's articles, bylaws, and board-approved policies up-to-date and in compliance with legal obligations?

2. Does your church have mechanisms (e.g., internal audit) to ensure operations adhere to relevant policies, laws, and regulations? Are these compliance activities well-resourced and empowered to function effectively?

3. Do board members and staff annually sign and honor conflict-of-interest policies?

# *Prayer*

Father, thank You for allowing me to serve You through my board service. Thank You for the church and for each and every person who is a part of it. Help me to do my part to ensure we are a church that exemplifies grace and forgiveness. Help us to take care of Your church and the people who You send our way. Help us to protect them as You have instructed us in the model prayer You taught us all, "protect them from the evil one" (John 17:15 NIV).

# *chapter ten*

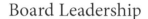

## Board Leadership

There is a difference between mediocre and exceptional boards. Some would argue there is no reason for mediocre board members. If a church or ministry is experiencing mediocre boards, it is simply because people do not know what it means to serve as a board member, the board chair does not know what it means, and no one is teaching the people what it means to serve as a board member. It is time for the nominating, board development, or governance committee to have the conversation at the board level. Encourage orientation, training, and a process of changing the culture of mediocrity in the boardroom.

Whereas exceptional boards model a deep commitment, add value, and advance the mission of the organization, oftentimes in faith-based organizations when questions of clarification, addressing challenges, or constructive debate happen, these actions can be misconstrued as a board member being obstinate or having an agenda. This assumption is not fair not only to the board members who are fulfilling their due diligence, but it also reflects a board culture that is not forward-thinking or strategic in what matters most to the success of the organization.

Wanting to be a board member that reflects exceptional boardmanship should be the goal of everyone who agrees to serve as a board member. Board members reflect a spirit of collaboration, engagement, trust, and respect with one another and the leaders of the organization. This cannot help but affect the outcomes and overall health of the organization itself.

We find ourselves circling back to the motivation question: why do board members serve? In my denominational tribe, when it comes time for the annual board elections, people start getting nervous. They know or sense that they might be getting the proverbial phone call, letter, or water cooler conversation that says, "You have been nominated, selected, or asked to serve on the board [elder board, etc.]." Some people react like they just received the letter to serve on a jury! They gasp, moan, and cry; some get ecstatic or give a sarcastic response that reflects their true Christian feelings! As a result, some church leaders have moved away from the nominating process to a recruitment process. They choose board members who might align with their vision or who would become the rubber-stamp board. After all, it is not spiritual to vote no when doing the Lord's work! How do we recruit and disciple (more on this later) board members who want to serve because they realize serving is their true act of worship?

In Romans 12:1 (NIV), we find these words: "Therefore, I urge you, brothers and sisters, in view of God's mercy, to offer your bodies as a living sacrifice, holy and pleasing to God—this is your true and proper worship."

As a Christian education professor, I often tell my colleagues, "Christian education professors do not exegete. If we do exegete, we did not mean to exegete!" When we use the term *exegete,* according to King and Powers (2021), "the exegete should seek an understanding of what the author is attempting to communicate to the original audience through the text. Ultimately, the focus of exegesis is to comprehend the inspired message revealed through the Scripture passage." As I write and consider what Paul is saying to the Christians in Rome, I find myself put in a place to do what Christian education professors do not do: exegete a passage of scripture. My colleagues would be so proud!

Let us dive in, and if you think this will preach, please feel free to use this in your next sermon! Just do not plagiarize! Ha! Ha!

Romans 12:1 (NIV): Therefore, I urge you, brothers and sisters, in view of God's mercy …

Paul is continuing his remarks from the previous section, where he has reminded them that salvation has come for both the Jews and Gentiles. Paul is writing to everyone who has identified as a follower of Christ—those who call themselves Christians. This gift of salvation is from God and is for anyone and everyone who believes.

… to offer your bodies as a living sacrifice …

Thanks be to God that because of Christ's death and resurrection, we no longer have to offer beasts or material things on the altar for our salvation. All Christ commands from us is our lives totally surrendered and committed to Him. Diehl (2022) states it this way: "Presenting or yielding our bodies to God speaks of a crisis and a process … a gift and a life."

… holy and pleasing to God …

We are no longer living to please ourselves. We have died to our selfish selves (Galatians 2:20). Christ is more interested that we live completely committed to Him, as this pleases Him. He is not interested in half-hearted Christian living. He set the example for all of us by giving His all; He simply asks us to give our all, in living and serving Him.

… this is your true and proper worship.

As we live for and to please God, we find ourselves in a position of using our spiritual gifts (1 Corinthians 12:4–5) and begin living out the fruits of the Spirit (Galatians 5:22–23). In using these gifts, we begin to walk in unity with others in the body of Christ who are doing the same. The church functions best when everyone utilizes their unique spiritual gifts. Discipleship is not practiced alone.

What would happen if board members begin to see their service as an opportunity to use their spiritual gifts and to be engaged in discipleship? I realize that some of you thought discipleship only took place when there was an official Bible study session. As we look at how Jesus recruited, developed, and interacted with the twelve, we certainly can see discipleship taking place in their lives. Leaders, instead of bemoaning the board member selection or election process, should see this as an opportunity to engage these individuals in discipleship, help them discover their spiritual gifts, and live out those gifts as they serve the church or organization. Board selection, election, or the nominating process should be promoted as an opportunity to grow in their faith and help the church fulfill its mission. We must train these individuals on true board governance and emphasize the spiritual component of serving. We just might have more people saying yes to serving than running away from the opportunity. There are many reasons people serve on boards, ranging from the desire to give back to increasing the size of their professional network. Can you help bring the joy back in serving? After all, it is their "true and proper worship."

Leadership now more than ever is being scrutinized and evaluated. There are challenges leaders are facing in the faith-based world that are unprecedented. There are issues and pressures on outcomes, measurements, accountability, and financial matters. Leaders are required not only to focus on internal organizational forces, but external forces are part of the equation as well. With this added pressure, boards are looking for leaders with various leadership and management styles and the skill of leaders to navigate the organization and staff through these challenges successfully. Some leaders have proven themselves successful in navigating themselves, their staff, and the organization as a whole through these perilous times. For others, pressure has become too much. Research has shown that approximately two-thirds of senior-level leaders are planning to switch positions within the next seven years. The apostle Paul reminds us to conduct ourselves in such a manner and be people who reflect being transparent, sincere, truthful, and genuine and have integrity.

There is no room for abusive power in the church or boardroom. What there is room for are servant leaders. Those types of leaders who focus on the needs of others carry a strong sense of accountability for their own thoughts, actions, and words.

# Pause and Reflect

Take a moment to reflect on what scripture has to say about serving as a board member. Space has been created for you to write your responses to the questions asked in this section.

**True and Pure Worship**

> Therefore, I urge you, brothers and sisters, in view of God's
> mercy, to offer your bodies as a living sacrifice, holy and
> pleasing to God—this is your true and proper worship.
> —Romans 12:1 (NIV)

You have been nominated, selected, elected, and set apart to serve the church through your board service. In this service, your reality must be to serve Him and to do His will, and as you do, you will know He is pleased. It's nothing more and nothing less than this simple truth.

# *Think about It*

1. Were you made aware of the spiritual and financial health or background of the church, its history, staff, board members, committees, etc.?

2. Why do you want to serve on this particular board, and do you consider yourself a leader?

# *Prayer*

Father, here I am, ready to serve You. You have chosen me for such a time as this. Thank You for the opportunity to worship You through my service.

# *chapter eleven*

## Roles and Responsibilities
## of the Board

There are many roles and responsibilities in serving as a board member. In the past, serving as a board member may have been viewed as a cushy role with no additional responsibilities other than attending the required number of meetings, hearing and approving reports from staff committee members, and of course hiring and firing the senior pastor or executive director. In today's fast-paced world, the role of the board is changing and expanding. Board members are finding themselves engaged in monthly update calls from the senior pastor or board chair and weighing in on technology, HR, finance, and other issues that oftentimes are not even related to the focus or purpose of the organization. Board members unwilling to devote the required time and effort to serve effectively should not accept the position or should resign from the board.

The days of recruiting, nominating, selecting, and electing board members based on criteria whereby someone is not qualified or does not clearly understand the roles and responsibilities, or might be stuck in generational thinking, *We have always done it this way,* may not be the best board practices. Perhaps in the vetting process, the nominating committee needs to look at potential board members based on their expertise in technology, finance, HR, marketing, discipleship, or evangelism. A board member who can help ministry leaders see the bigger picture is a valuable asset. Perhaps the nominating committee looks for individuals who come from different backgrounds or have different perspectives than other board or staff members. Again, helping them see or gain a different perspective that can be easily overlooked. It is almost impossible to make board training too basic. Even simple topics, such as how to make motions, ask questions, and how business flows through committees, are important for new members to understand. This is in addition to getting them to serve the right committee that aligns with their strengths. Notice this last sentence. It is not a process of assigning individuals to committees because we have always had committees and someone has to serve on the committee. What would happen if we moved to a strategy of allowing people to choose the committee on which they want to serve, based on their interests, strengths, and expertise? Caution has to be given here on the potential for conflicts of interest, especially if there are staff members assigned to the committees as well. The board members serving on the committee are just this: committee members. They are not wearing board member hats and cannot be biased or show bias when it comes to the committees they are serving. A best practice might be to rotate members through committees so they spend time knowing and understanding the other areas of the ministry and eliminating polarizing factions or potential silos.

Just the mention of the word *committee* gets people really nervous, anxious, and jittery. But just as you have learned not to get nervous about the fiduciary responsibilities, the same can be said about committees.

Committees are subgroups of the board. Their tasks have been identified and outlined by the board, and the committee does not work outside the parameters of what the board has established. It is important that a board member serve as the chair of the committees. This action gives the indication that the work of the committee is in alignment and under the guise and direction of the board.

Traditionally, boards in faith-based organizations found themselves serving on one of the following committees. You were either viewed or assigned as a steward, trustee, or Christian education committee member. Individuals serving on these committees shall never meet or talk! Depending on the cultural needs of the church, one committee usually held more power than the other. In reality, it is more about a board dividing itself into committees to carry out its assigned responsibilities. In some instances, the bylaws and laws of the state in which the church or ministry is located dictate how the board can be elected and organize itself. Whatever needs the organization has determines ongoing or standing committees. Some committees are time limited. If it is determined your church or ministry needs committees to carry out its work, then it is imperative that the following questions guide the committee selection and process:

1. Do we need this committee?
2. What are the roles and responsibilities of each work group?
3. How do we set up our committees for success?
4. Who should serve on our various committees?
5. How do we assess our committee's effectiveness?

Committees have a purpose and can contribute to a board accomplishing its work and needed tasks. It allows and enables board members to use their expertise in ways they often cannot do in regular board meetings. It is important for their success and positive contribution to the work of the board that the committees be set up and used appropriately. Annual evaluation and flexibility allow the board to address any potential conflicts or structural problems or issues with the committees themselves or members.

## COMMITTEES AND CONFUSION

Have you been assigned to a committee in your board member role? Committees have a purpose in the life of the organization unless they are rooted in traditions and have lost their relevancy where the organization finds itself today. Are the committees helping or hindering the work of the board?

Remember in the chapter on board recruitment we discussed the importance of recruiting board members with expertise, skills, and experiences that will contribute to keeping the organization moving forward. This same principle can be applied when assigning board members to the needed committees of the board. Not all the work of the organization has to or needs to be relegated to a standing committee. Most churches have the following standing committees:

- finance
- education
- evangelism/discipleship
- executive committee

Oftentimes, other activities that can be handled or addressed by time-limited task forces would suffice versus a standing committee and causing another meeting that board members have to commit to attending.

As organizations experience change, oftentimes committees' tasks get easily lost or forgotten about or their work is left undocumented. Undocumented committee work contributes to the confusion of who is responsible for what, and confusion leads to conflict. To prevent confusion and conflict, it serves the organization well when establishing committees to appoint someone to record minutes so that the board is unified on the number, function, and authority of the committees.

Because of the confusion of committees, the best approach would be to eliminate committees. Depending on the size of the organization, eliminating committees could contribute to the organization's inability to meet its mission. Committee members in smaller organizations serve and contribute to the management of programs and people. Therefore, committees may be vital to the success of the organization. Do not be too quick to throw the baby out with the bath water. Healthy boards evaluate the usefulness of committees and make adjustments to committee uses and structures as needed.

Consideration needs to be given to what is often referred to as standing committees. These are usually the finance, executive, and governance committees. Maintaining standardized committees ensures consistency in overall board practices.

As stated earlier, in most faith-based organizations, you will find the trustees and stewards committees.

## TRUSTEES

Primary responsibility for setting the policies of the Christ-centered organization rests with the members of its governing board. For good reason, they are often called "trustees" because they are charged to hold in trust all of the resources given to them by God.

## STEWARDS

The word *stewards* conveys the same meaning but with biblical roots. In the original language, *stewards* meant "householders" who managed all of the affairs of the household. The term makes a clear distinction between ownership and stewardship. While everything belongs to the owner of the household, the steward owns nothing. Yet the owner (God) trusts the steward with the management of all. The biblical definition of a steward determines the role of the board in every facet of its governing role. A steward owns nothing but manages everything.

Serving and giving board leadership means being aware of the legal responsibilities board members have. Some boards are quick to answer they have directors and officers insurance that covers any legal ramifications that may be encountered. This type of insurance and coverage is very important to have, as board members can be held liable for failure to perform fiduciary duties or fulfill legal requirements. This insurance is applicable for nonprofit, profit, churches, and faith-based organizations.

Having clear guidance and training on ethical practices not only protects the board member but the churches and ministries themselves. It is the responsibility of the entire board to ensure that the organization conducts its financial affairs in accordance with legal and ethical

# *Pause and Reflect*

Take a moment to reflect on what scripture has to say about serving as a board member. Space has been created for you to write your responses to the questions asked in this section.

## Accountability

So then, each of us will give an account of ourselves to God.
—Romans 14:12 (NIV)

Is accountability a part of the language of the board in which you are serving? Do board members hold themselves accountable for the success or even the failure of the organization? What does accountability look like? If the organization is not experiencing growth or seeing positive results, could it be the responsibility of the current board? Could it be because the board is weak and ineffective? There are numerous case studies where board members have hired and fired executive directors while thinking this will bring about the needed changes in the organization. In reality, the problems that exist within could be the board members themselves. Perhaps it's time for the board to take a look at their governance structure, make the necessary adjustments in which they govern, and watch the needed changes become a reality without a revolving door scenario around the executive director's chair. When it comes to the end, it is the board as a whole that is held accountable for everything the organization does and what is accomplished.

# *Think about It*

1. How engaged is the board in reviewing the IRS 990 Form?

2. How often does the board review and update the conflict-of in policy?

3. How often does the board review and approve an independent a

4. When does the board approve the annual budget?

5. Does the board engage in an annual retreat?

6. Is there an annual review of contracts and licenses and other le agreements by either the board or staff?

7. Is there an annual review of the organization's investments a policies guiding or taking into account any major changes in tl investment climate?

8. How often are the bylaws reviewed?

9. Does the board engage in an annual or periodic assessment o evaluate its own performance?

10. Does the board verify that the organization and staff are still focused on the strategic plan put in place by leadership?

# *Prayer*

Father, *accountability* can be an intimidating word. It also can be a word that brings a spirit of freedom into our lives. Help us to live our lives in such a way that is open, transparent, and allows others to see we are not hiding, conniving, and pursuing our own agendas and we are seeking what is best for others. Today, I give You permission to search me and to know my every thought, motive, and desire as a board member. May You find a board member who is first seeking You with all their heart, soul, and mind. Then may You find a board member who is seeking what is best for the organization in which You have called me to serve. My prayer today is that You find a servant with an open heart and hands and who is not afraid to be held accountable.

# chapter thirteen

## Board Recruitment

You are probably asking yourself as you looked at this chapter heading, "When did the recruitment of board members become a part of my job?" Best practices state that board recruitment is the responsibility of every board member. And some might even refer to the bylaws that indicate how board members are recruited, selected, elected, and vetted. My challenge to those involved in the process of recruiting board members is to ask, "What would happen if the thinking was changed to not just trying to fill open board positions but finding the best individual with the right blend of skill sets, expertise, community connections, and sphere of influence?"

As ministry leaders, one of the most important jobs is to always identify potential volunteers and leaders to help carry out and fulfill the mission. Again, I refer to Romans 12:1 (NIV). "Therefore, I urge you, brothers and sisters, in view of God's mercy, to offer your bodies as a living sacrifice, holy and pleasing to God—this is your true and proper worship." We are in the process of looking and giving individuals opportunities to worship God through their acts of service. And I believe serving as a board member is and can be an act of worship.

So in case some of you think I am suggesting you become a renegade and bypass your bylaws in the nominating procedures, please take time to review and follow your organization's bylaws. What would happen if in the nominating process you began the board recruitment strategy with a more focused approach not limited to but including the following?

- doctrine check
- faithfulness check (attendance)
- giving check

In the strategic planning process, you identified if the church or ministry is going to need HR, technology, real estate, or programmatic expertise. Again, following the recommendations of your bylaws, the nominating committee begins looking at potential board members who have expertise in the needed areas and who meet the additional criteria as described above. You now have a strategy in place that moves the nominating process away from filling holes to filling board positions with clearly defined expertise and bringing relevance to the strategic planning and the needed decision-making. You also have identified and connected with leaders and stakeholders who see a reason for their service as board members.

Some recruitment processes solicit candidate suggestions from staff, committees, and board members. Notice I did not say *recruit* potential board members. The reasoning for allowing the staff to nominate is that the staff is engaged with volunteers and has identified and vetted ministry leaders to help them in their ministry endeavors and programming. If a staff struggles with identifying potential board members, then it might be time to evaluate the staff members' leadership and influence on their own volunteer recruitment strategy. There is no reason for being a Lone Ranger in ministry. Some have phrased it this way: "Even the Lone Ranger had Tonto." This can be translated to mean that you should not be doing ministry alone. Could the Lone Ranger take care of the bad guys by himself? Yes! He was a trained and qualified

Texas Ranger. He and his horse, Silver, rode all over the countryside confronting and taking care of the thieves, thugs, killers, and mean people. Then along came Tonto, the loyal and trustworthy companion to the Lone Ranger. They discovered they really did need each other. In your ministry assignment and tasks, you need those volunteers, and they need you.

Another suggestion to enhance the importance of what it means to be recruited and to serve on the board is look for individuals who have been serving on committees and vet them through with the chairs of their respective committees to be certain of their capabilities to serve the ministry objectively and with faithfulness and passion.

After individuals have been nominated, invite the nominees to an interview with the ministry leaders and/or board chair. This gives both the nominee and ministry leaders an opportunity to share the vision, mission, and strategic plan with the board candidate and to hear their own hearts or concerns for the ministry. In addition, it gives ministry leaders an opportunity to identify or raise cautionary flags of any negative influence on the board or ministry as a whole, if this particular candidate's name should continue to be allowed to remain on the ballot. If, after going through the vetting process (however described in the bylaws), the decision to allow their names to remain on the ballot is up to the candidate, at least they now are a little more informed about what it means to serve on this particular church or ministry board. Utilizing a board matrix (http://www.buildabetterboard.com/board-matrix-worksheet/) is a helpful tool to help identify potential board members with the needed skills, talents, and abilities. The board matrix is also used to identify what present skills and abilities are present in your current board. The matrix will help the ministry decide where it wants to go and who is needed to help get it there.

Some ministries and organizations are using a nominating or board development committee. Identifying and recruiting potential new board members should be the responsibility of the nominating committee to ensure an adequate supply of qualified individuals. Well-written and established recruitment policies and procedures used and reviewed regularly will enable the assessment of current board members' expertise and identify gaps. Engage in personal interviews to screen candidates, and allow for performance assessments of incumbents. Keep in mind the board recruitment process is not a once-and-done initiative or strategy. It is ongoing. This is why some ministries and organizations have relegated this ongoing task to a governance committee. Recruitment is continuous, with the members always identifying and cultivating new candidates.

The goal of establishing a board recruitment strategy is to create a successful board. It is time to end the annual struggle of the year to identify and recruit new board members. It is possible to make the board recruitment process an enjoyable and rewarding discipleship-making experience.

# Pause and Reflect

Take a moment to reflect on what scripture has to say about serving as a board member. Space has been created for you to write your responses to the questions asked in this section.

## One Body

For just as each of us has one body with many members, and these members do not all have the same function, so in Christ we, though many, form one body, and each member belongs to all the others. We have different gifts, according to the grace given to each of us. If your gift is prophesying, then prophesy in accordance with your faith; if it is serving, then serve; if it is teaching, then teach; if it is to encourage, then give encouragement; if it is giving, then give generously; if it is to lead, do it diligently; if it is to show mercy, do it cheerfully.
—Romans 12:4–8 (NIV)

Paul is reminding the believers that they have been given gifts for the good of the body, gifts such as encouraging, leading, showing generosity, and sharing the gift of mercy. It is important to note that not everyone has all the gifts or the same gifts. We all have been given different gifts. The purpose of these gifts is to serve the church. We serve fellow Christians by loving and lifting each other up. When was the last time you took a spiritual gifts inventory assessment? When was the last time the board took a spiritual gifts inventory assessment? Some boards spend an extraordinary amount of time discovering their leadership strengths. This is not a bad thing or idea to do. What would happen if a board would not only assess the leadership strengths but assess the spiritual gifts of individuals as well? By the end of the day, we just might have the right people serving out of their gifts and strengths and meeting the needs of the church.

# *Think about It*

1. How should a board react to an unsolicited request from an individual who wants to serve on the board?

2. What are your strategies for board recruitment?

3. How can the board make board roles more attractive to both current and prospective board members?

# *Prayer*

Father, thank You for the gifts You have given me, and thank You for the leadership skills You have given me as well. I want to use these in my role as a board member. I often find myself wondering what I bring to the board table or role. I look around and see people who are much smarter or more eloquent than I am. I second-guess myself a lot. But I know You have a purpose and reason why I am in this role. Do not let me buy into Satan's lies and make me feel like I have nothing to offer. I want to serve, and I want to be here. Here I am, hands wide open, ready, and willing to serve You through the gifts, skills, and the abilities You have given me.

# chapter fourteen

## Board Orientation

D o you know that perfect cup of coffee you pick up from your favorite coffee shop? You do realize that whoever made that cup of coffee for you had to be trained or go through some form of orientation? They did not show up one day, fill out an application, get hired, receive an apron, and get told to get after it! Well, at least you hope this was not the case. No, your barista was trained on the when, who, what, where, why, and how to make their brand of coffee that meets the standards and quality of their company's mission and purpose. In case you missed it, the barista went through orientation and training. Orientation has purpose and meaning.

The foundation of a committed, knowledgeable, and effective board is orientation and education. As an essential companion, every organization should have a thorough board manual that board members can use throughout their terms.

A board manual serves two functions. For the new board member, it is an orientation handbook that provides useful information about board structure and operations. For the balance of a member's service, the manual becomes an indispensable working tool and a central resource. Materials can be added and removed to create an up-to-date reference. Many organizations find it beneficial to begin the program year with a board orientation session or sessions.

Orientation is not a once-and-done proposition. Board orientation happens every year as new board members are elected, and the need for orientation is ongoing.

Some organizations have moved the responsibilities of the board member orientation to that of the governance committee. Having a designated governance committee reiterates the message to both new and incumbent board members about the importance of board development and orientation. Having an established policy requiring mandatory board orientation will contribute to strengthening board performance.

Failure to provide training and poor recruiting habits plague many organizations. It is time to move away from being frustrated with nonperforming board members or bemoaning the process and make board development, training, and orientation a priority and give it the attention it deserves.

Board orientation should include, but not be limited to, the following:

- roles and responsibilities of board members to meet the organization's mission and programs
- structure of board and staff
- strategic plans
- financial reports (current and a few years back)
- committees and job descriptions and goals

The orientation manual or handbook can provide a helpful and historical perspective on what the previous board had been discussing and the issues and decisions the church is facing. The manual should focus on essential pieces of information that a new board member needs to bring them up to speed as quickly as possible. In addition, the manual will include

- bylaws
- policies
- board and staff relationships
- committee structures, list, role, and chair
- current operating budget
- copy of current financials
- most recent 990 Form and financial audit or review
- dates of board meetings for the current year
- current board roster (including contact information and roles for all board members)

Taking the time to put together a board orientation manual can seem overwhelming. The premise of this book is to have board members who contribute successfully to the church and to their service as board members. It is imperative, for a board member to be effective, that he or she fully understands the organization, its goals, and how they as individuals can help achieve those goals.

You want board members who will read the packet and not get bogged down in hundreds of useless pages of information that is read by few and useful to no one.

One of the most important messages that should be communicated to board members before, during, and after each board meeting is that the board speaks as one voice outside the boardroom. As a board member, there will be opportunities for discussion, debate, and decision-making. Each board member should take responsibility for maintaining a level of professional decorum and focusing on the issue being discussed versus personalities, seeking clarification, and being willing to accept the board's decision after having an opportunity to speak. It is never appropriate or acceptable for a board member to speak against a decision made at the board level outside the boardroom just because the decision did not go his or her way. The dissent should be voiced openly in the board meeting and during the debate. The negative vote should be recorded in the minutes, and the other board members should respect the dissenting board members' vote. A dissenting vote does not indicate or should not communicate a message of a board member not being a team player. The goal is to affirm and encourage one another inside and outside the boardroom. We are not striving to be a board that suffers from what has been identified as groupthink.

In reality, we are talking about the emotional intelligence (EI) of individuals and groups. EI speaks to the ability to self-manage and ability to relate to others.

At this stage of board orientation, the goal of the board should be seen as working as a team. Effective boards exemplify the virtues of respect, trust, and candor that all speak of what it means to serve as a team and to be a team. Each of these virtues builds on one another.

A healthy board functions as a team. Knowing and understanding the roles and responsibilities of what it means to be a board member and meeting the expectations of being a board member is a daunting task. There is a spirit of congeniality and recognition of individual differences. At the same time, if the differences become behaviors that interfere with the board getting its work done, there must be action taken, as directed by policies, to remedy the situation so the board can focus its attention on its duties and responsibilities.

# Pause and Reflect

Take a moment to reflect on what scripture has to say about serving as a board member. Space has been created for you to write your responses to the questions asked in this section.

## The 12 Disciples

When morning came, he called his disciples to him and chose twelve of them, whom he also designated apostles: Simon (whom he named Peter), his brother Andrew, James, John, Philip, Bartholomew, Matthew, Thomas, James son of Alphaeus, Simon who was called the Zealot, Judas son of James, and Judas Iscariot, who became a traitor.
—Luke 6:13–16 (NIV)

It is interesting to read the account of Jesus's choosing the twelve disciples. The custom that day was for a student to approach a rabbi and ask to be taught or mentored by him. But as we often see Jesus do, He turned the tables and did the approaching or choosing of those He wanted to follow Him and become His disciples. He spent time with them. He trained them. He instructed them. He gave them opportunities to go do what He had taught them to do. He believed in them. The book of Acts reflects that the twelve did what they learned by watching and participating in the ministry of Jesus. The twelve graduated from Jesus University (not meaning to be sacrilegious with that title)!

Jesus still is calling boys, girls, men, and women to follow Him. He is still using people to impact the world! We need more graduates who are willing to learn, go, and do the work and ministry of the master teacher.

# *Think It Through*

1. Do new board members receive an effective orientation to the nonprofit's work, organization, and board responsibilities?

2. How do you convince a new member to go through orientation if he has already served on numerous boards and feels he understands what board service is all about?

3. What does it look like when a board engages in groupthink? What are the pitfalls of such behavior? What are some techniques for overcoming groupthink?

## *Prayer*

Father, thank You for calling me into my role and service as a board member. For some reason, You see something in me that I quite honestly do not see in myself. I am humbled by this opportunity as I imagine that some of the twelve were. Help me in my board service to act and live humbly, serve graciously, and act wisely.

# *chapter fifteen*

## Integrity

One would think that addressing the topic of integrity and how it relates to board members and their service would be a total waste of time, ink, or pages. We can learn what it means to be a man of integrity from looking at the life of the apostle Paul (Acts 23:10–21). Paul was a man who

- spoke the truth in every situation
- lived in line with scripture
- kept a blameless conscience before God and man

As we think about being board members who lead with integrity, we can know that integrity leads to credibility. When we think of individuals with integrity, we usually think of characteristics, such as being open, trustworthy, honest, and consistent in speech and action. These are not bad traits to possess and exemplify to our friends, fans, and family, right?

How do we measure a person's integrity or hold a board member accountable for the integrity they show in the boardroom and with their fellow board members? Here are four ways to measure boardroom integrity:

- quality of discussions at board meetings
- credibility of committee reports
- use of constructive professional conflict
- degree of knowledge and engagement in all matters related to the board business

It is imperative that both incumbent and new board members have an understanding and be prepared to meet the expectations of their own performance (ethics, integrity, commitment, accountability, and development). Board members have many functions as has been identified in and throughout this book. And because of their many roles, it takes more than having a passion or enthusiasm for the cause or mission; it certainly goes beyond good intentions. There has to be a clear understanding of responsibilities, and a demonstration of integrity in fulfilling duties, and everything is done for the organization.

Being an organization that leads with integrity is not something that should be taken lightly. Accountability is a concept used quite frequently in and throughout scripture. The Evangelical Council for Financial Accountability (ECFA) provides for its members who want to be held to a higher standard and held accountable to what they call "The Seven Standards of Responsible Stewardship." Organizations joining or partnering with ECFA are expected to comply with all the standards.

# Pause and Reflect

Take a moment to reflect on what scripture has to say about serving as a board member. Space has been created for you to write your responses to the questions asked in this section.

## Accountable to God

The LORD does not look at the things people look at. People look
at the outward appearance, but the LORD looks at the heart.
—1 Samuel 16:7 (NIV)

Accountability to God is vital, but people form their impressions of both people and organizations by looking at outward appearances. Thankfully, God does not look at the outward appearance but at the heart of man.

What makes people tick? My wife and I sometimes are in a crowd of people and see someone dressed a little bit differently, responding out of the norm, or acting strange. My wife and I look at each other and almost say in unison, "I wonder what their story is." Everyone has a story. The good news is our stories become richer and with greater purpose and meaning once God gets involved. He wants to be involved in our stories. He has been working on our stories since the beginning. He knows us and loves us. He has seen us at our best and seen us at our worst. The psalmist reminds us in Psalm 139:1–4 (ESV),

> O LORD, you have searched me and known me! You know when I sit down and when I rise up; you discern my thoughts from afar. You search out my path and my lying down and are acquainted with all my ways. Even before a word is on my tongue, behold, O LORD, you know it altogether.

If this does not keep your thoughts, actions, and attitude in check inside and outside the boardroom, then perhaps spending some time asking the Lord to change and transform you might be a good first step in having Him involved in your story.

# *Think It Through*

1. What are the board's role and responsibility for setting the organization's culture of integrity, values, and philosophies?

2. Is there a code of conduct that governs the behavior of board members, management, staff, and volunteers? Is the code understood and reflected in the policies?

3. Is the board satisfied that stakeholders' concerns have been adequately addressed and that their interests have been incorporated into the organization's code of conduct and other value statements?

4. Does the organization encourage an environment in which information is exchanged freely while respecting confidentiality? Does an atmosphere exist in which people feel they can ask questions openly?

5. Do the board and leadership set an example in exhibiting their commitment to the organization and its success?

6. Does the board demonstrate integrity, credibility, trustworthiness, active participation, ability to handle conflict constructively, strong interpersonal skills, and the willingness to address issues proactively?

## *Prayer*

Loving Father, thank You for this warning not to rely on outward appearances, knowing that the heart of man can be so deceitful. Help me to keep my mind fixed on Jesus so that in all I say and do—it may be the life of the Lord Jesus that flows out from me—so that I may be pleasing in Your sight. In Jesus's name I pray.

# *chapter sixteen*

---

## Unity and Maturity in the Body of Christ and in the Boardroom

---

As we continue our discussion on all things boards, we are going to be applying the principles of truth we find in the passage found in Ephesians 4:1–16 over the next few chapters. You are going to be amazed to discover how scripture speaks to what it means to be a board member who works in unity with one another and who reflects maturity in his board service. You will also be amazed how the Ephesians 4 passage has so much application to board service.

When it comes to doing the business of the church, it is easy to fall into the temptation to divide rather than focus on what unites us. We are people who are walking and living by the Spirit. As we live and serve Christ and others, our devotion to and for Christ should be evident in our behavior and how we express that devotion and behavior. In and of ourselves, we are not worthy of this high calling, but thankfully Christ does not see us as we are but as we could be. This does not mean He still does not rebuke, convict, correct, discipline, and forgive us. He knows us and sees us as individuals. And He loves us enough to change us.

As you serve as a board member, remember this is not about you. Yes, you bring your gifts, skills, abilities, and personality to the boardroom or table. But take a look around the room. Do you see others sitting around? Do you realize these individuals have gifts, skills, abilities, and personalities as well? It is a beautiful thing when all the individuals come together with each of their unique characteristics and work in unity and for the good of the church or organization. Your pastor and board chair need you to work in harmony and unity to accomplish the work God has called them to do. As you serve your fellow board members by listening, yielding, and engaging in the greater good versus what you think or feel, then you are fulfilling and living out your calling. And once the members of your congregation hear the board is working together, this sends a message that will resonate through all the cracks and crevices of the church, and the message will be communicated, conveyed, and circulated near and far.

# *Pause and Reflect*

Take a moment to reflect on what scripture has to say about serving as a board member. Space has been created for you to write your responses to the questions asked in this section.

## Unity and Maturity

> As a prisoner for the Lord, then, I urge you to live a
> life worthy of the calling you have received.
> —Ephesians 4:1 (NIV)

Paul is reminding the early church and believers we are to serve Christ as one body and in unity. Using our gifts to build up the body and be people who have recognized the calling, gifts, and blessing to be a part of the kingdom of God.

Reality tells us that because the church is made up of people, there are going to be times we may not agree with one another. But we must remember we are the body of Christ. We must reflect on unity as we serve one another, seek peace with one another, and reflect on the one hope we all have found in Jesus Christ. As we live out this hope and calling, it will show up through our behavior, attitudes, reactions, and actions. Our prayer should be that we find ourselves worthy of the calling that Christ has for each of us.

# *Think It Through*

1. How does the board acknowledge the differing points of view of its own members and demonstrate respect for dissenting opinions?

2. Are there challenges that the church is facing right now that require unity?

3. What steps can be taken to ensure a spirit of unity permeates in and through the life of the church?

## *Prayer*

Father, as I think about the calling You have placed on my life to serve as a board member, I cannot help but think how important it is to be a board member who seeks peace and unity in the life of the church.

# *chapter seventeen*

## Be All That You Can Be
## in the Boardroom

I love reading the "be" verses found in Ephesians 4:2–3 (NIV).

> Be completely humble and gentle; be patient, bearing
> with one another in love. Make every effort to keep the
> unity of the Spirit through the bond of peace.

If you want to know how to behave in the boardroom, this is a good place to start. Is this a new revelation for you to think you are going to have to be humble, gentle, patient, or one (unified)? Especially as you think about serving as a board member in a church or faith-based organization. One would think of all places that people would be, that this just would not be necessary. As a professor who teaches a group and organizational behavior college course, about midway through the course every semester, I read a student's response that goes something like this: "I never realized that in this course we would be talking about people's behavior in organizations." Whether we're talking about management and leadership behavior or employees' behavior, it doesn't matter the title you have or earned or did not earn. People will be people, and there are lots of reasons why people will be people. You can spend an extraordinary amount of time trying to figure out the ifs and whys of people, but the best strategy in dealing with people is first to learn how to manage yourself.

- What makes you tick?
- What are your strengths and weakness?
- How do you manage change and conflict?

Once you have this figured out, then you can learn to manage and lead others. Some people are quick to hand out what I call a spiritual Band-Aid to explain people and their behavior. We hear such comments as the following:

- This is just who they are.
- God made them that way.
- They always have been that way.
- Someday God is going to get a hold of them and change them.

I do not want to diminish the power of prayer as we pray for these individuals who seem to show up in the boardroom or for sure have a leadership role in the life of the church. We should pray for them. At the same time, we need to learn how to manage their behavior and lead them to be all that God wants them to be.

Keep in mind as you manage and lead others that Jesus gives clear instructions on how to be successful in this endeavor. In Matthew 7:3–5 (NIV), we read,

> Why do you look at the speck of sawdust in your brother's eye and pay no attention to the plank in your own eye? How can you say to your brother, "Let me take the speck out of your eye," when all the time there is a plank in your own eye? You hypocrite, first take the

plank out of your own eye, and then you will see clearly
to remove the speck from your brother's eye.

Here's the message: manage yourself first and manage others second. How does your life line up with the "be statements" found in the Ephesians passage?

In case you think I missed the last part of that verse, it's "bear with one another." Some people like to keep the "be" part going and add or change it to "be a bear" in the boardroom, in the life of the church, to the pastor and leadership. I would encourage you to read that verse again and make sure you are reading and getting this right. As you are living out the "be" verses, you soon will find yourself knowing and understanding what it means to bear with one another. Again, not excusing away bad behavior or giving out spiritual Band-Aids, but living out your life in front of those who have yet to discover what it means to be all that God wants and intends for them to be.

# Pause and Reflect

Take a moment to reflect on what scripture has to say about serving as a board member. We have created space for you to write your responses to the questions asked in this section.

## Be Worthy

Be completely humble and gentle; be patient, bearing
with one another in love. Make every effort to keep the
unity of the Spirit through the bond of peace.
—Ephesians 4:2–3 (NIV)

We were created for community. Living in community as Paul describes in this passage doesn't mean we become communal people. I love some of the people in my faith community, but I just could not live with them! The gifts, skills, and talents that God has given me are to be used in community to build up the body of Christ. I can serve others by using these gifts. As I serve others, my own spiritual faith will grow. Paul is inviting us to know and experience Christ through the involvement and in the lives of other believers. This passage is written for the believers. As we learn to live and serve our fellow brothers, then we can serve those who do not know Christ. As they say, it all starts at home or in your own community.

# *Think It Through*

1. How or what does the church reflect the vision Paul describes in these verses look like?

2. Does the church body reflect people who are gentle, humble, and patient with one another? If not, what can the leadership or church board do to ensure this happens, is taught, or is emphasized?

3. What is it about our structure, processes, policies, and procedures that unifies the church, the board, and the staff?

# *Prayer*

Jesus, You prayed for the unity of the believers in Your high priestly prayer. You modeled for us what it is to be one with the Father and You asked the Father that those who have and are following You would continue to be one. It is out of being one with You and with one another that the world can believe in You.

# *chapter eighteen*

## Unity of the Spirit in the Boardroom

As a believer or follower of Christ, your life reflects different values, beliefs, and behaviors from those who are not followers of Christ. In your board member service, there is a difference between a board member who serves on a for-profit board and a nonprofit board.

Though both for-profit and nonprofit board members have a passion for the organizations in which they have agreed to serve, there are different motivating factors for their services. These relate directly to the differences between for-profit and not-for-profit boards. These differences include board structure, duties and responsibilities, financial reporting, mission, and usually board member compensation.

Here's the charge Paul is exhorting the believers in Ephesus, Colossae, Laodicea, and other churches in the area: because you are followers of Christ and have identified as believers, then seek peace and unity with every member of the body of Christ. It is a pretty tall order and not to be taken lightly or not always easy to carry out. Why? The church is made up of people. And people sometimes pursue their own agendas, act, react, and respond in ways that do not always reflect the unity of the Spirit or anything that looks remotely peaceful. Oftentimes, this response is seen in the church sanctuary, hallways, fellowship hall, atrium, parking lots, choir loft, choir rooms, boardrooms, pastor's office, youth and children's ministry areas, and the list goes on! What would happen though if a board decided that its response to one another in this room, and at this time, would always reflect the peace, love, and unity of Christ? One of the ways we demonstrate love and forbearance of other board members is by acknowledging the differences of opinion, considering others' points of view, and always assuming we are striving for a common goal.

Yes, there are going to be times of dissent and difference of opinion in a board meeting. A board member should never feel afraid to express a dissenting viewpoint or that an opinion is not valued. This is where the board minutes are so important and the minutes should reflect the dissent with noted reasons. It is important to note that a dissenting vote does not mean you are not a team player or are being obstinate. A dissenting vote reflects a board member fulfilling his due diligence. Board members are allowed and encouraged to ask tough questions, but they are not doing it for the sake of causing dissent. Best practices suggest creating a culture of positive dissent in the boardroom. It behooves a board member to live out the charge given by the apostle Paul in Ephesians 4:3 (NIV). "Make every effort to keep the unity of the Spirit through the bond of peace." A board member who is voting a dissenting vote just out of control or anger issues (resolved or unresolved) must be dealt with by the stated policies and given an opportunity to continue to help the church move forward in a positive fashion or agree to step aside so that the church can continue to move forward. In conflict management in the life of the church, it is always advisable to use the biblical model of conflict resolution found in Matthew 18:15–21.

# *Pause and Reflect*

Take a moment to reflect on what scripture has to say about serving as a board member. Space has been created for you to write your responses to the questions asked in this section.

## Unity and Peace

> Make every effort to keep the unity of the
> Spirit through the bond of peace.
> —Ephesians 4:3 (NIV)

Did you know that having peace with others contributes to having a peaceful relationship with the heavenly Father? It can be viewed as being both a vertical and horizontal relationship. Have you ever tried to pray while angry with someone? Perhaps Psalm 139:23 (NIV), "Search me, God, and know my heart; test me and know my anxious thoughts" might have implications for ensuring that our vertical relationship is in sync with God, before we try living and loving our fellow brothers. It is interesting that these two characteristics of unity and peace show up and go together. You cannot have one without the other. Do you want unity and peace in the boardroom? Then do your part to bring it. Do whatever it takes to ensure it shows up and is evident in every aspect of the business of the board and in your actions as a board member.

# *Think It Through*

1.  How does the Spirit help maintain the "bond of peace" with others in the church?

2.  How unified is the church, the board, and the leadership team?

3.  Is it OK to have differences in the boardroom or in the church? How would Paul encourage you to respond to these differences?

4.  According to the wording in verse 3, is Christian unity to be a prime or secondary goal for us?

## *Prayer*

Father, may I be a person who brings peace to a chaotic and restless world? May I be a person who reflects peace as I interact with my fellow brothers and sisters in Christ? May I be the peacemaker, a unifier, and a leader who brings the team together, listens well, and serves and brings joy to You.

# chapter nineteen

## One

In my faith tradition, there is significance to the sacrament of water baptism. It signifies to me and to the witnesses of my baptism that I have confessed my sins to Christ, I believe that Jesus Christ is Lord, and that through the act of worship, I am becoming one with my Lord and Savior. Baptism has significance and meaning not only for me but for other believers as well. It makes my bond stronger and the unity with them sweeter. I no longer live for my own selfish reasons. I am living a life that seeks and keeps the unity of Spirit with others.

What would happen if board members took this same thought, idea, and philosophy into the boardroom? The decisions made, the discussions, the reports, the business of the church, and personal feelings and agendas were set aside, and the bond of peace took over and unity of the Spirit became the focus. Would it make a difference? Would meetings become more focused and productive?

As I write this, we are living in a world that is reflecting division on every topic, issue, and political arena, no matter what side of the aisle, color, or animal. It seems like everyone is on edge. The sacred has become a battleground. The world does not look the same, and I have often wondered, *Could we be living in the last days as prophesied in the scripture?* Because we are people of hope, we cannot lose hope or communicate a message of hopelessness. At the end of the day, even with all the dissenting voices that seem to be shouting louder and louder, the believers must unite and proclaim our message of hope that we serve "one God and Father of all, who is over all and through all and in all" (Ephesians 4:6 NIV).

It is imperative that board members keep the church moving forward and be a voice of unity. There are still people who need to hear the life-changing message of Jesus Christ. The church still has a voice in a world that is trying so desperately to drown it out. We need board meetings that reflect the business of the church, but we also need board meetings where board members are praying for and with each other. Sharing and hearing reports of people who have found and discovered new life through a personal relationship with Jesus Christ, our hope, the one who brings salvation, and is Lord over all and through all. We need to equip and train board members to talk about Jesus versus what the church is or is not doing. The board needs to hear reports from ministry leaders that reflect people coming to Christ and repenting of their sins, getting baptized, and becoming disciples and followers of Christ. The board needs to hear stories of how people are talking and telling their neighbors, coworkers, and everyday people they are meeting (from the coffee barista, Uber driver, and the fast-food workers) about spiritual conversations they are having and having an opportunity to pray and lead these individuals to a personal relationship with Jesus Christ. The board needs to handle requests or recommendations from the finance committee for an increase in the evangelism budget as evangelism ministry expands or explodes within and outside the walls of the church. The board spends an extraordinary amount of time defining the meaning of evangelism and what it means to evangelize and needs to spend more time reading the biblical account and Jesus's strategy to evangelize his world. And the great news is He instructed us to go and do what He did. This is the business of the church. Nothing more and nothing less.

# *Pause and Reflect*

Take a moment to reflect on what scripture has to say about serving as a board member. Space has been created for you to write your responses to the questions asked in this section.

## The Doctrine of Unity

> There is one body and one Spirit, just as you were called to one
> hope when you were called; one Lord, one faith, one baptism; one
> God and Father of all, who is over all and through all and in all.
> —Ephesians 4:4–6 (NIV)

God's way of doing things always amazes me and goes beyond what I could ever think or imagine (Ephesians 3:20). In Ephesians 4:4–6, we find seven "ones" passages. The number seven represents perfect and holy. This is reflected in who God is. As we live out these seven "ones" found in this passage, we will find they will shape how we interact with others.

The oneness does not divide us; it unites us. It shapes our thoughts, words, and decisions. Perhaps there is a person, family member, or coworker where the relationship could be better. Instead of focusing on all their faults and what they have done or did not do, take a look within and confess your own sin and shortcomings. You may not be able to change others, but with God's help, you can change your own heart and attitude. Remember this is not about you. It is about maintaining a spirit of unity with your fellow brothers and family members.

# Think It Through

1. What do you do if there is a disagreement in the board?

2. What do you do when there is a disagreement between staff and the board?

3. How should the board handle divisions from the body of Christ? Should they just tolerate them?

## *Prayer*

Father, thank You for Your holiness and for modeling for us how we are to live with one another. Please help and forgive me for those times that my spirit does not reflect the One I call Lord and Savior. Help me not to have to win every battle and certainly not to die on every mountain. Help me bring unity to the conflicts and peace to those things and situations that can easily divide us.

## chapter twenty

## Spiritual Gifts in the Boardroom

H ave you ever taken a spiritual gifts inventory assessment? If not, I would encourage you to do so. For some, it can be a very eye-opening experience. For others, you will discover the aha moment of why you do what you do and enjoy doing what you do, and it is all because of the gifts God has blessed or bestowed upon you. Here is the good news about spiritual gifts: They are given for a reason, which is to build up the body. Look around your church. Are people using their gifts? If not, why not?

A few years back, there was a trend in church life to become a staff-driven church. As a Christian educator, when I first heard about this strategy, I threw a yellow penalty flag (that's for all the football fans out there) and started quoting Ephesians 4:11–13 (NIV).

> So Christ himself gave the apostles, the prophets, the evangelists, the pastors and teachers, to equip his people for works of service, so that the body of Christ may be built up until we all reach unity in the faith and in the knowledge of the Son of God and become

mature, attaining to the whole measure of the fullness
of Christ.

I felt better, but I'm not sure anyone really heard my cries or saw the yellow penalty flag, except my wife, who just shook her head and encouraged me to keep teaching and ringing the bell of "equipping the saints." After taking a few steps back, reading a few books and articles in trying to understand this movement, and the trend in churches becoming staff led, I finally realized that some churches actually were living out Ephesians 4:11–13. They were equipping the saints for works of service. They were letting the professional staff train teams of volunteers in carrying out the various ministries of the church. Now this I can sign off on and get on board with. Allowing one person to handle multiple responsibilities stifles the growth of the church. The mission should drive everything you do. It takes a team of paid staff and volunteers. This was the model that Jesus gave us. Remember the twelve He chose to help him? We need to learn from one another, listen to one another, be sensitive to one another, and realize it is Jesus who brings us together.

Discover your spiritual gifts and how you can use those as you serve the church. Are you allowing others to discover and use the gifts that God has bestowed upon them? Remember the body needs these individual gifts to function.

Christ has established the local church as a place where believers can discover and exercise their spiritual gifts.

Do we do a disservice to our fellow brothers and sisters when we do not recognize or give them an opportunity to use their spiritual gifts for the good of the body of Christ? God calls and equips leaders from within our congregations. Hopefully, you are in your position of leadership because someone gave you an opportunity to use or recognize your spiritual gifts. As I have often quoted to volunteer ministry leaders, the church needs you and you need the church. God wants to take the church to new places, and He has always used people to do the work and carry out His plans. We need to recognize those He has gifted and help fulfill the plan God has for His church.

# Pause and Reflect

Take a moment to reflect on what scripture has to say about serving as a board member. We have created space for you to write your responses to the questions asked in this section.

**He Gave Us Gifts**

> But grace was given to each one of us according to the measure of Christ's gift. Therefore it says, When he ascended on high he led a host of captives, and he gave gifts to men.
> —Ephesians 4:7–8 (NIV)

Have you realized what truly the gift of salvation is? Paul is reminding the church in Ephesus that they or we all have received a gift of grace. When we look up the definition of *grace,* we will find it means "getting something we don't deserve." It is through this gift we can have and experience unity (which Paul seems to address a lot in his Epistles as he writes to the various churches) in the body of Christ.

We do not have to focus on our differences. If we use the gifts Christ has given each one of us, the body of Christ can and will experience unity. We each have been given different gifts, and these gifts are to be used to build up and equip the church. The focus is not to be on who or what gifts each one has but on how to use these different gifts for the good of the church. Let us help others realize that first, the gift of salvation has been given to everyone. Second, Christ has bestowed upon everyone various gifts to equip and build up the body of Christ, and third, as we use these gifts, others might come to know and receive the gift of salvation.

# *Think It Through*

1. How would your church be different if every member viewed himself or herself as a servant with a ministry to fulfill?

2. Have you helped others discover their roles or created opportunities for individuals to identify and use their gifts in the life of the church or organization?

3. What systems does the church have in place to identify the various roles needed to build up the body?

# *Prayer*

Dear Jesus, as I look around the boardroom table, I want to give You thanks that You have extended the gift of salvation to every one of us around this boardroom and in our church. It is a gift that we do not deserve, but we are thankful You have bestowed it upon each and every one of us. May our mission, vision, and focus always be to extend and proclaim Your gift of grace to anyone and everyone.

# *chapter twenty-one*

## Speaking the Truth in Love
in the Boardroom

I have been around the church long enough that when someone begins "speaking the truth in love," I get a little nervous, especially when the conversation begins with "Now what I want to share with you is out of love" or "Please understand this conversation is not meant to harm you or cause you any problems. It is because I love you." It reminds me of my growing up days right before my dad had to remind me in his love language what "speaking the truth in love" really meant! If you have served in church ministry as a pastor, paid staff, or volunteer ministry leader, you know how those conversations can go and, more importantly, how they feel. The person having the conversation usually feels better than you do after having it. But remember it was "done in love."

When the conversations in the boardroom move in a direction that has to be addressed "in love," this is the time to start looking around and pulling out the notes of personality tests, enneagram types, assessments, and conflict resolution strategies. You will begin to see a shifting of chairs, notes, bodies, and facial expressions. Some are appalled by such behavior taking place in a faith-based boardroom. Others are relieved that the elephant in the room is finally being addressed. Remember it is not about avoiding conflict; it is about managing conflict. It can be awkward to raise accountability issues with others inside and outside the boardroom.

Being transparent or speaking the truth in love does not allow or give permission for the board or anyone in a leadership position to be abusive or, as apostle Peter wrote in 1 Peter 5:3 (NIV), "not lording over those entrusted to you, but being examples to the flock."

Healthy boards allow for civil and honest discourse. I realize in today's political landscape and even in everyday relationships (work, play, education, neighborhood, etc.) that a healthy discourse has become an anomaly.

Faith-based boards have an additional source to help navigate them through the naysayers or challenging conversations and decisions. This is relying on the power of prayer. The board members should be praying for their leaders, each other, and for protection as they give leadership and shepherd not only themselves but the church as a whole. Is it evident in the way you handle yourself, challenges, or even maybe the people sitting in and around the boardroom that you have taken the time to pray for them? Have you taken the time to pray for your own attitude before stepping into the boardroom? Are your responses and reactions evident of one who has spent time in prayer? Prayer can make a difference.

# Pause and Reflect

Take a moment to reflect on what scripture has to say about serving as a board member. Space has been created for you to write your responses to the questions asked in this section.

## Speaking the Truth

The one who has knowledge use words with restraint,
and whoever has understanding is even-tempered.
—Proverbs 17:27 (NIV)

We need more people who know when to speak and when to be quiet. We need more people who measure their words carefully, to be people who use their words in a way that builds up versus tears down, instills confidence, and encourages others. People who are insightful and use discernment as they speak. Jesus once again models for us on controlling our speech and tongue when we would rather respond with emotion. As Jesus was standing before the Roman rulers, being accused of crimes He did not comment, He held his tongue. He was a man of self-control. Many think a person demonstrates power when the person stands up for their rights and does not take anything from anyone. But greater is the man or woman who relies on the Holy Spirit to give them strength and power to be an individual who reflects self-control than one who speaks quickly and foolishly to prove to himself and those around him that he is nothing more than a fool and absent of emotional intelligence.

# *Think It Through*

1. Why is it important that we learn to control what we say?

2. What are some ways, both positive and negative, our speech might impact others?

3. When is it wise for one to keep silent? When is it unwise?

## *Prayer*

Father, the words to the familiar Psalm 19:14 come to mind today as I pray.

May these words of my mouth and this meditation of my heart be pleasing in your sight, LORD, my Rock and my Redeemer. (Psalm 19:14 NIV).

Thank You, Lord, for the reminder that You know me and You know the words I will speak even before I speak them. Thank You for the gift to speak. Help me not to take advantage of or misuse this gift. Help my words be a source of encouragement, help, and most of all, to offer up praise to You.

# *chapter twenty-two*

## Dealing with Difficult Board Members

The first thing we have to do as we broach the topic of dealing with difficult board members is to define what we mean by *difficult*. Difficult can look, feel, and sound different just from whoever is in the room or sitting in the chair. The goal in managing group and organizational behavior is not necessarily to eliminate conflict or bad behavior but to learn how to manage it. Some of the ways in which bad behavior, conflict, or difficulty show up in the boardroom have been identified.

- When individual board members push or pursue their own agendas based on their own interests or positions on important issues that may not be shared by others.
- Engaging in water cooler conversations or parking lot meetings outside regular board meetings to manipulate or plan how to have their positions on issues presented or approved at the board meeting.

Take a look around the boardroom. Are there board members that you would classify as difficult? Board members who create tension at meetings? Make meetings unpleasant? Have you ever walked away from a board meeting wondering when the board chair was going to address this renegade board member? Is it possible to have a board member who might be considered difficult but does not keep the work of the board from getting done? Some board members might be considered as single-issue members who want to highjack every meeting to focus on their pet projects or personal agendas. Others might simply be overbearing or contrary for the sake of provoking discussion.

The strategies in dealing with these types of board members include prevention, containment, or ultimately removal.

The apostle Paul has identified the characteristics and competencies that are needed for elders in the church (Timothy 3:2–7 and Titus 1:6–9). As we read through the list of characteristics, we would be hard-pressed to read, "Be obstinate, difficult, and overbearing." What we do find are characteristics that affirm and serve others. It is a matter of modeling behaviors that reflect Christ in who we are and what we do both inside and outside the boardroom. This is the time to do some self-evaluation and measure your ability to

- be sensitive to others
- have the ability to take time to listen
- be a servant leader
- be a team player
- have clear focus on the vision, mission, and a positive perspective
- celebrate the success of individuals and the church

As a leader, your role is to help or contribute to the development of the personal competencies of your board members, staff, or fellow team members. This means taking the time to train, focus, and develop these competencies to result in changed behavior, not only in individuals but also in the organization as a whole. At the same time, changed behavior has to be an internal motivating factor.

# *Pause and Reflect*

Take a moment to reflect on what scripture has to say about serving as a board member. Space has been created for you to write your responses to the questions asked in this section.

## What Causes Quarrels among You?

> What is the source of wars and fights among you? Don't they
> come from your passions that wage war within you?
> —James 4:1 (CSB)

How do you respond to those coworkers or family members who just seem to know what buttons to push to engage you in frivolous arguments and topics?

It appears that James has to address the early church on proper and respectful behavior toward others (inside and outside the church). It seems that there was what I like to *term a whole lot of stone throwing* (judging) going on between believers and nonbelievers. But why? James is reminding us it is time to take a spiritual inventory of our own lives. What is going on within us? Could our outward actions or reactions toward others be because of the war going on within us? Have you ever tried to pray for someone with whom you are angry? It usually does not work out too well. If you are like me, as you are praying for them, you begin to tell God why you are angry with this particular individual and rehash all the wrong they have done toward you. Then you forget why you were praying, and while you are down in your praying position, you just decide to pick up another stone and identify the wrong that has been done or said and you justify in your own heart why it is OK to throw it! You have been treated wrong, unfairly, unjust, and unkind, and you are going to get even! I think James is simply telling us to put down the stones, take a step back, figure out what is going on, and respond not out of selfish desire but out of love, compassion, and with a spirit of forgiveness.

# *Think It Through*

1.  Are all conflicts wrong? If not, when and how can we know that we are fighting for the right cause, not for sinful reasons?

2.  Do the bylaws or policies contain any wording about treating people with mutual respect, courtesy, etc.?

3.  Do the bylaws or policies include or mention how to resolve unacceptable behavior of board members?

# *Prayer*

Father, help me not to become a stone collector and label each of the stones with those things that have been said, done, or made me respond in ways that do not reflect a man who walks with and by the Spirit. I guess if I'm going to collect stones, I should label them with those individuals I need to pray for and figure out ways I can encourage these individuals. It is out of Your power that I can pray and lift others up. Help me not to trust in my own skills and strength but to trust in You, the One who can and will help me love people as You love them.

# chapter twenty-three

## Strategic Planning

Here is another $64 million question: who is responsible for the strategic thinking and planning for the church or ministry? Does it fall to the pastor, executive committee, staff, or board? It's incumbent on the board to address strengths, weaknesses, opportunities, and threats every year. Every organization faces challenges, demands, and opportunities. Strategic planning addresses each of these components and ensures the church is responding and not reacting to the needed changes. This process prevents churches from being caught unaware of the changing environment around them and allows them to make needed adjustments.

When was the last time the board meeting reflected time spent in strategic thinking and planning? When boards spend time in the strategic thinking and planning process, it should be an exciting time for both staff and board members. It gives them an opportunity to dream together and share how to achieve that dream! Here are some key thoughts to keep in mind:

- History has a way of bringing out the naysayers in the process.
- It is an exhausting process.
- It is a process that will have to be repeated as new leaders (staff and board) change and are added.
- Dissent and conflict can be diminished, addressed, and resolved.
- Focus on the importance of the process and its benefit to the church and/or ministry.

As we continue the discussion on board governance, there is a need to help guide board members in understanding their roles and responsibilities in the organization's strategic planning. The following four strategic planning questions guide the board members in the strategic planning process.

Having the board engaged in the strategic planning or vision casting process allows the board to know where the organization is headed. It is aware of the strengths, weaknesses, and opportunities that exist both internally and externally for the organization. It can be prepared to deal with unexpected situations that may arise.

Strategic planning moves the organization beyond just letting things happen. It ensures the organization is moving forward with purpose in meeting its mission and purpose. As an organization changes and grows, it will experience many life cycles that require different leadership skills and talents to navigate. The important strategy for leadership to address is to identify where in the organizational lifestyle the organization finds itself and responds accordingly. Strategic planning is dynamic and certainly not static. It requires deliberate thinking, planning, and a periodic review.

The pastor, staff, and board should be involved in the strategic planning process. To relegate this responsibility to a committee diminishes the board's role and responsibilities in governance. The board leads in the strategic planning process from the perspective of listening and learning from the staff and stakeholders and looks to the senior pastor for insight to ensure the church is offering programs and services that reflect the priorities of the church. It does not have to be a complicated process. Remember the strategic planning process is not about recasting the vision or mission of the organization or identifying the values of the organization. The strategic planning process is identifying where you are and how you will get from here to there.

# Pause and Reflect

Take a moment to reflect on what scripture has to say about serving as a board member. Space has been created for you to write your responses to the questions asked in this section.

## The People Rebel

All the Israelites grumbled against Moses and Aaron, and the whole assembly said to them, "If only we had died in Egypt! Or in this wilderness! Why is the Lord bringing us to this land only to let us fall by the sword? Our wives and children will be taken as plunder. Wouldn't it be better for us to go back to Egypt?" And they said to each other, "We should choose a leader and go back to Egypt."
—Numbers 14:1–4 (NIV)

Oftentimes in leading a church, faith-based organization, or any organization, when things are going great and the milk and honey are flowing freely, the people are content. Things begin to get a little uncomfortable when there is a budget shortfall, a transition in staff, or the stakeholders are asking questions of board members that cannot be easily answered. Everyone looks to the leader and they want answers, or they are quick to point and throw blame, complain, and grumble just like the Israelites did with Moses and Aaron. Wise is the leader who stays strategic and reminds the board members of the vision and mission of the organization. The leader remains focused and calls his team together, and they strategize and navigate through the disruptions and conflicts. The leaders lead with a clear purpose and enthusiasm and continue to communicate the vision that keeps the people both inside and outside the organization excited and engaged.

# Think It Through

1. Where does the board see the church or organization in the next year?

2. Has the organization participated in a SWOT analysis (strengths, weaknesses, opportunities, and threats)?

3. When was the last time leaders revisited the vision, mission, and values of the organization? Is there a need for a change in any of the areas?

4. What are the strategic priorities for the organization? (Try and limit it to one to three goals.)

5. What are the goals for three, five, or ten years from now?

6. Are the goals SMART (specific, measurable, achievable, relevant, and time bound)?

# *Prayer*

Lord, thank You for allowing me to lead this group of people. I certainly do not feel qualified for such a task. It can be overwhelming, daunting, and tasking! I can relate to Moses as he led the Israelites out of bondage to the Promised Land. Sometimes it feels like all I'm hearing are the complainers and naysayers. Just as You provided help for Moses by giving him a group of elders to help carry the load, You have given me a group of elders, board members, and committee members who are helping to carry the load that we are facing in our organization or church right now. Help our vision to be Your vision. Help us not to be dismayed or lose heart. Help us realize that the Promised Land is just around the corner. We are not in this battle alone. For that I am thankful. As Your spirit was with Moses and the seventy elders, Your spirit is with our leaders and me.

# *chapter twenty-four*

## Conflict in the Boardroom

Conflict in the church is not new. The early writers had to address church conflict, dysfunction, and unhealthy behaviors in their various letters to the early church. The church is made up of people, and these people are all at different points in their journey of faith. There are some who are mature disciples, there are immature Christians and people with problems, and there are non-Christians attending the church as well. A healthy church will reflect dysfunctional, conflict-prone, and ego-driven individuals. And this is the church as God wants it to be. Remember people are not looking for the perfect church. They are looking for a church that reflects people who are real, with real struggles, and who are who they say they are. A healthy church is not void of conflict but is a church that seeks to resolve conflict.

What happens when the conflicts spill over into the boardroom or among the leaders? This is where the leader, whether this is the senior pastor or the board chair, has an opportunity to be a servant leader. A servant leader loves and leads those individuals who may not always be easy to lead or love. The leader taps into their emotional intelligence and encourages the board members to do the same. It is not about who is right and who is wrong. It is about connecting with and listening to people, to offer kindness and empathy, and to lead and display patience. It is being a leader who models integrity, compassion, and forgiveness.

## HEALTHY CONFLICT VERSUS UNHEALTHY CONFLICT

Yes, you read this right. There is such a thing as healthy and unhealthy conflict. Endeavoring to stay on the positive side of things, we will begin with looking at healthy conflict and what this means for the board. There will be times in the boardroom when the agenda will contribute to different perspectives on certain decisions being considered by the board. Having different opinions and perspectives is not a bad thing. It is often out of the differing opinions and perspectives that a more effective and efficient solution will come to the surface and move the board to a unified decision versus one individual acting alone. This kind of conflict is usually healthy and should be acceptable and encouraged.

Unhealthy conflict occurs when relationships become strained and people and feelings become secondary to responding as Christ responds to each of us. There will be times of tension, frustration, and difference of opinion in the boardroom; the goal is not to divide and draw lines in the sand. The goal should always be reconciliation, keeping the mission in mind, and staying focused on the same page.

As a board, the goal is not to avoid conflict but to manage it. If a board does not experience some form or type of conflict, then it might be time to spend some time in evaluating the board's transparency with one another, its health, and its ability to serve as a board that exemplifies servant leadership toward one another.

As leaders, time might need to be spent during orientation on how to engage in conflict in the boardroom. Just as some individuals go into marriage not knowing how to handle conflict, these same individuals might find themselves caught off guard when conflict shows up in the boardroom. Successful conflict resolution includes

- forgiveness
- justice
- repentance
- reconciliation

# Pause and Reflect

Take a moment to reflect on what scripture has to say about serving as a board member. Space has been created for you to write your responses to the questions asked in this section.

## Cultivate Respect for Each Other

> Be completely humble and gentle; be patient, bearing
> with one another in love. Make every effort to keep the
> unity of the Spirit through the bond of peace.
> —Ephesians 4:2–3 (NIV)

What is the trust and respect level like within your board? Is there a culture of respect, trust, and candor with one another? As a board, it is imperative that there be a development of mutual respect, trust, and the ability to share difficult information, challenge one another, and respond and adjust individual responses by asking intelligent questions of one another.

Perhaps this is what Paul was asking the church of Ephesus to reflect on a culture of mutual respect, trust, and candor with one another. And above all, love one another. Respect can go a long way and shows up as we take the time to listen, learn, and love one another. Have you ever noticed how often the word *love* is used in Ephesians 1, 3, 4, and 5? It is a common theme.

- God chose us in love (Ephesians 1:4).
- We should be rooted and grounded in love (Ephesians 3:17).
- We should bear with one another in love (Ephesians 4:2).
- We should speak the truth in love (Ephesians 4:15).
- We should build up the body of Christ in love (Ephesians 4:16).
- We should walk in love (Ephesians 5:2).

Paul is encouraging us to not only love the loveable people but also the difficult people in our lives. After all, "by this everyone will know that you are my disciples, if you love one another" (John 13:35 NIV). I do not know a better place to practice loving one another than the boardroom. Maybe getting it right there will help get it right in the workplace, home, and wherever life finds us.

# *Think It Through*

1.  Which of the three statements most accurately describes you and/
    or your church's approach to conflict?

    *   I/We usually avoid dealing with conflicts even though everyone
        knows they are there.
    *   I/We usually deal with conflicts in a way that drives people
        further apart.
    *   I/We usually deal with conflicts in a way that results in resolution
        and reconciliation.

2.  Are you satisfied with the way conflict is managed in your church?
    Can you give examples of how conflict is used to improve the quality
    of decisions? Or how it is harming relationships?

3.  How does authority flow in the church?

# Prayer

Father, thank You for showing me that conflict is not new to the church. Help me to be a peacemaker when conflict does arise. Help it to unite us rather than divide us as a board. Help me step out of the way, learn to listen with both ears, and not be quick to speak. Help me to be a voice of encouragement and to serve from a position of one that uplifts my fellow brothers and sisters and certainly not one that tears down. Help me not to be afraid of conflict but to learn to manage it to keep the mission moving forward.

# *chapter twenty-five*

## Navigating Difficult Issues

No one ever expects problems, crises, or issues with organizations, but as we all know, life happens, and the unexpected happens. The rhetorical question that should be asked at this juncture is this: what does the organization do, or how does it respond when problems or crises happen? Basic business strategies dictate that the best way to deal with a crisis is to anticipate it.

As we discuss this topic of crisis management, let us look at some of the areas that could contribute to crises and best practices on how to manage the crises. First, there should be set policies in place on how and who is going to respond to the crisis or even the potential of a crisis. If a committee has been designated by the board to address potential crisis management and response, then great care should be taken to ensure any and all legal matters have been considered.

No organization ever plans on facing fraud, financial loss, or the need for children and youth safety protection from sexual abuse or perpetrators. Certainly, no one ever thought the pandemic of 2019 would affect the world, church, or individuals as it did. If the pandemic taught us anything, preparing for the unexpected required churches and nonprofit organizations to respond in different ways.

Churches expect members to get along and differences of opinion to be civil and respectful. Unfortunately, countless stories could be told where division and differences of opinion have resulted in legal action among parishioners, pastors, and board members.

When there is a crisis within the organization, oftentimes everyone looks to the leaders of the organization and asks the proverbial question "Who is in charge, and how did this happen?" Three preventative strategies can help guide an organization through the crisis.

1.  Communication. The CEO, director, senior pastor, board chair, and board have to ensure there is clear, open, and transparent communication so no one is caught by surprise or off guard when there is a crisis.
2.  Training and development. Board members need education and training. It is important to provide training for new board members to familiarize them with their duties and responsibilities. It is not enough to know about good governance, but it is acting and being aware when there are warning signs of potential crises in the organization.
3.  Red flags. Board members need to watch for and be sensitive to a culture that avoids tough questions of leadership. As board members, their responsibilities include asking questions, requiring answers, and expecting evidence. To take a lackadaisical approach in holding the leadership accountable shows a lack of trust. Ignoring these responsibilities fails to hold the leadership accountable.

It is often during a crisis that questions are being asked by stakeholders, perhaps by the media or individuals outside the organization. It is imperative that the board has a crisis and communication policy in place. The policy should include the staff's and board's roles, and communication strategies are clearly defined. It must be clear to board members and staff that only those designated by stated policies or appointed by the board are spokespersons for the church or organization.

Managing and responding to a crisis is somewhat like managing conflict, as discussed in chapter 21. There are correct and incorrect ways to respond to and manage a crisis. The wise leaders and board will ensure there is a crisis plan in place. At this juncture, one is probably asking what type of crisis organizational leaders should be prepared for and how they should respond to a potential crisis, such as

- criminal activity
- data breach
- misappropriation of funds
- natural disaster
- child safety issues

Best practices would suggest that there is an appointed crisis management team that has been trained, instructed, and equipped to walk through any crisis or potential crisis that the organization may face.

Some board members will avoid the crisis or some will even resort to resigning from their board positions. In counseling circles, we would call this the fight-or-flight syndrome. This is a response to stress, and for some when there is a crisis, their tendency is to combat the stress with a fight-or-flight response. It is important not to ridicule or diminish the value of these individuals and their response to the crisis. One has to consider that this is their defense mechanism and how they have learned to cope, respond, or avoid stress in their lives.

It is important that the leadership responds, guides, and is present during the crisis the organization is facing. If the organization has a definite plan and set policies in place to guide the organization (board members and stakeholders) through the crisis, this should be viewed as an opportunity to strengthen the organization and ensure its ability to continue to thrive and meet its mission.

# Pause and Reflect

Take a moment to reflect on what scripture has to say about serving as a board member. Space has been created for you to write your responses to the questions asked in this section.

## Disruption

> A few days later, when Jesus again entered Capernaum, the
> people heard that he had come home. They gathered in such
> large numbers that there was no room left, not even outside
> the door, and he preached the word to them. Some men came,
> bringing to him a paralyzed man, carried by four of them.
> Since they could not get him to Jesus because of the crowd,
> they made an opening in the roof above Jesus by digging
> through it and then lowered the mat the man was lying on.
> —Mark 2:1–4 (NIV)

In this passage, we find Jesus doing what He loved doing best: spending time with people. He was teaching and healing them. It was just who Jesus was and what He did! Wherever Jesus was, the people wanted to see Him and to hear what He had to say. And in this account, we find Him in Capernaum in a house that probably could only hold a very small amount of people. The people were standing by windows and doors and on top of each other. They wanted to hear and see this man called Jesus! There was a paralyzed man who could not get in the house or even close enough to Jesus to be healed by Him. But he had four friends who could and would get him to Jesus so their friend could be healed. They were determined, and they were willing to do anything for their friend. So they climbed on top of the house and started digging a hole through the roof.

As we read this story, we see that there are religious leaders observing Jesus and doing everything they can to catch him so they can arrest him for blaspheming or doing something against their teachings. And Jesus does not disappoint. His first action is to say to the man who has just been lowered through the roof of the house, "Son your sins are forgiven." You know the religious teachers, when hearing these words come out of Jesus's mouth, just about sent them into a moment of unsanctified anger. In reality, it just added to the case they were building against Jesus. And then Jesus performs the healing miracle. This same man who came through the roof walked out the front door!

What I find amazing about this story, Jesus was amazed at the paralyzed man's and his friends' faith. Jesus also knew that man had a greater need than physical healing. Jesus saw the man's sinful heart. God always knows and sees the heart of a person and the real need of individuals.

Challenges, disruptions, and conflicts always seem to show up, and they seem to show up when we're the least prepared. Faith and determination are sometimes all we have left as we navigate through the challenges or disruptions. It is a process of recognizing that God will provide and meet the need. His provisions may seem out of the norm. He may use people, circumstances, and situations, but He is always there waiting, willing, and able to meet the need of the hour. And sometimes when we present our needs to Jesus, He looks deep within and not only meets the immediate need but meets needs known and unknown.

# Think It Through

1. What are the emergencies and controversies that could affect our organization?

2. Where is the greatest possibility for us to encounter a problem?

# *Prayer*

Father, I often find myself praying, "There is nothing that happens that catches you by surprise." I truly believe that statement. I have prayed it countless times. But I'm not sure the same can be said for the organization in which I find myself serving as a board member. There are some things and situations that do catch us by surprise, unprepared, and not sure how to respond. As leaders, we have to balance all of our responses in a clear, logical, and yes, even legal manner. We want to be good stewards of the organization. Help us not bury our heads in the sand and take the approach or attitude "Nothing bad is going to or can happen to us." Help us to be prepared to the best of our abilities. It is far better to be proactive than reactive. May You guide us as a board to prepare for the worst, have a plan for action, and remain calm and in control if a crisis occurs.

# *chapter twenty-six*

## Trust

As we think about board behavior (ethical and unethical), we have to address it from the perspective of trust. Boards and organizations that do not reflect trust in their leadership and ensure there is a culture of trust throughout the organization do not function well. Board members must make a conscientious effort to ensure there are processes in place where accountability and trust are the acceptable norm for not only themselves but ministry leaders as well. Trust is an essential element of effective board governance. It is disconcerting to see trust missing from Christian organizations and churches.

It has often been said that leadership starts at the top. When it comes to creating trust within an organization, there has to be a trust-based relationship among leaders. This means from the senior pastor to the board chair and the board chair to the board. Successful organizations exemplify respect and trust and serve as each other's sounding board, champions, and yes, sometimes even, critic. It is a partnership that takes time to build and maintain, and it is built with intentionality.

In the annual board orientation, time should be spent on understanding the importance of trust amongst the leaders and board members. Trust is developed as board members learn to work together and grow as individuals and as a group.

If you had to evaluate the leadership of the board in regard to the focus of the board, would building trust receive high marks? Trust happens among the leaders, and as that trust is built, it affects donations, volunteerism, and board service, and in a faith-based organization, it is evident as board members' own faith grows and they begin to learn what it means to trust in God.

Trust inspires volunteerism and involvement as people desire to be part of something bigger than themselves. When there is an absence of trust from organizational leaders or from within the organization itself, it leads to frustration. To minimize these frustrations, respect and trust must be present in and throughout the organization, and the leadership and the board must model it.

The topic of trust cannot be addressed without looking at the behavior and characteristics of the leaders of the organization. Teams, stakeholders, and board members are looking for organizational leaders who model and exercise trust, lead with confidence, express confidence in team members, practice integrity, and above all else, are the type of leaders who can be trusted.

# Pause and Reflect

Take a moment to reflect on what scripture has to say about serving as a board member. Space has been created for you to write your responses to the questions asked in this section.

## Who Do You Trust?

Paul and Barnabas appointed elders for them in each
church and, with prayer and fasting, committed them
to the Lord, in whom they had put their trust.
—Acts 14:23 (NIV)

In this passage of scripture, we read an account where the known church planters Paul and Barnabas are in a position where they have to appoint "elders" to give oversight to the church. Do you see what we have unfolding here? We have Paul and Barnabas having to trust the newly appointed elders, and we have the new believers trusting the newly appointed elders. In case you missed it, that is a whole lot of trust going on in these churches. Paul's and Barnabas's responsibility is in planting and setting up churches, not in watering or pastoring them. This is where Paul gives further instructions on the qualifications of the elders of the church (1 Timothy 3:1–13; Titus 1:5–9). Yes, there are qualifications for leading the church, and these qualifications are clearly spelled out by Paul. Paul is trusting that God will equip the people from the churches to take on and give leadership so the churches can continue to thrive and grow. Paul will eventually return to these churches on his second and third missionary journeys. We find numerous letters written to the churches by Paul in the New Testament. These letters were filled with encouragement and instruction to the leaders and to the church as a whole. If you were to receive a letter from the apostle Paul today, what would the letter say? Would Paul find you worthy to be serving and giving leadership to the local church?

# *Think It Through*

1. Do your team members trust you?

2. Are you establishing a culture of mutual trust?

3. What can you do this week to cultivate trust with your people?

4. How would lack of trust between the board and the church leadership, board chair, or staff manifest itself? What would be the consequences for the organization?

# *Prayer*

Father, thank You for trusting me to serve and lead as a board member. As I lead, I simply trust that You will give wisdom where wisdom is needed. You will give grace, clarity, guidance, and peace as I walk and work along beside other board members who are striving to lead this organization.

# chapter twenty-seven

## Tell the Story

**A**re you passionate about being a board member? What motivates you to serve, attend a board meeting, serve on a committee, or share your expertise, knowledge, and skills? Are you seeing measurable results as the organization lives out its mission? Is anyone sharing or telling the success stories of the organization? Best practices tell us that every board member should be able to share at least two good stories about the impact in which the organization is having in the community, in their lives, or in the lives of others.

Everyone loves a good story! Storytelling is integral to a nonprofit's ability to advance its mission. Storytelling connects you to your community, stakeholders, and staff. In using storytelling, you are using it as a tool to make connections with your audience. This in turn makes the audience more likely to take action by giving, volunteering, or spreading the word about the organization. Organizations can utilize the following storytelling techniques:

- social media posts
- digital stories
- annual reports
- awareness campaigns

We will unpack these different techniques as we continue the discussion of utilizing good stories.

## SOCIAL MEDIA POSTS/DIGITAL STORIES

This strategy utilizes an approach that will not let a good story go to waste. Using highly visual and multimedia to share and tell stories helps the organization stand out from the crowd. Use your web site or other social media platforms to help tell your story, share the big picture (mission), and highlight individual stories. Keep in mind that the message must be crisp, clear, and compelling. The staff, board, and volunteers of the organization should be involved in the identification and collection of stories, as this is the responsibility of everyone. Having everyone involved creates a storytelling culture. Another strategy for creating a storytelling culture is to make stories an integral part of every meeting. Starting out a staff or board meeting with members sharing stories from those impacted by the mission of the organization gives credibility to the strategy of storytelling.

## ANNUAL REPORTS

Here is a news flash! Just the use of the words *annual reports* can cause some in the organization to mumble, grumble, and yawn! And respond with "Here comes the boring part of the meeting." It does not have to be this way. Taking the time to design a creative annual report that uses graphics, action words, and stories to highlight programs, people, and progress shows your target audience and the individuals reading and receiving the report that the organization continues to move forward and has a story to tell. Do not just rely on data to tell your organization's story in the annual reports. Utilizing stories in the annual reports will draw your audience into your world. Combining data with visuals helps tell the story effectively and clearly.

The one report that should not be boring is the treasurer's report. This report is sharing important financial information. Communicating the information clearly and in easy-to-understand language or graphics, tied into the mission of the organization, will keep your target audience and fellow board members engaged.

## AWARENESS CAMPAIGNS

Is your organization or ministry the best-kept secret in town? It does not have to be and should not be that way. Are you aware of what people are saying about your organization or ministry? Do you care what they are saying or what they know? Knowing, caring, and taking the time to market helps build the reputation of the organization. Yes, marketing can and should happen in the life of churches and faith-based organizations. What is important is to reach people where they have needs and where they feel pain and respond with the solution that the church can offer. Marketing is happening for the organization and church, whether you realize it or not. If there is a phone listing, signage, social media presence, or even a logo, guess what. You are marketing! The question now becomes this: how good is your marketing strategy?

An effective marketing strategy could make a difference in gaining new volunteers. It could also attract people who are seeking meaning, direction, and purpose in their lives. When people hear, see, and experience the services or ministry in a positive way, these individuals could become the voices that attract others, and you could begin to see people in your local community whose lives were changed because of the marketing strategies.

At this point, you are probably thinking, *Wait. When did marketing become part of my responsibilities as a board member?* If the premise of this book is true (and believe me, I do), then your service as a board member means you want to ensure the organization is successful and you are contributing to that success. How do you contribute to the success when it comes to the marketing strategy? It starts with the leaders asking themselves important marketing questions.

- Are people in our community aware of our church? Do they know we exist? How do we make them aware?
- Do our own people (members) show up for church services and events? Do we have special events that are attractive and show we are aware of our community and its needs?
- Do our members support the church and its work and mission financially?

Do not let the term *marketing* scare you, and do not be too quick to throw up a red flag and call this strategy heresy! If the goal for the church is to proclaim its message (life changing), then perhaps it is time to think outside the box, identify those with experience and expertise in marketing, and let us incorporate and allow these individuals to use their gifts to market the church!

Consider the budget for marketing, and before you know it, you just might become a board member of an organization that has its own web site, tweeting, Instagram profile, and more friends and followers on Facebook than ever thought possible! But remember leaders must ask themselves, "What is the goal for the marketing campaign or strategy?" It is OK to have a marketing strategy that helps give people a glimpse or view of who and what your church is about. It is OK to be engaged in the community by participating in events that give the church opportunities to introduce members of the church to the community. Investing in the marketing strategy will more than likely start seeing your church marketing efforts pay off! Having a focused strategy in place can help your church grow and impact the kingdom of God in ways you never thought possible!

# Pause and Reflect

Take a moment to reflect on what scripture has to say about serving as a board member. Space has been created for you to write your responses to the questions asked in this section.

## How Will They Know?

> But how can they call on him to save them unless they believe in him? And how can they believe in him if they have never heard about him? And how can they hear about him unless someone tells them? And how will anyone go and tell them without being sent?
> —Romans 10:14–15 (NIV)

Here's a biblical passage that is speaking marketing language and giving us a strategy before marketing was trendy and cool! Jesus once again is showing us that He uses people to communicate the message of hope and salvation to a lost and dying world. He has commanded us to go into our world and tell. In the twenty-first century world that you and I live in, it does not necessarily mean selling all of our possessions, going to language school, and boarding a plane to go to a third-world country. Going into the world these days could mean going into YouTube, Facebook, the internet, down the street, into the workplace, or community and reach, teach, and preach the Word right where we are. The message you know and have experienced needs to be told. Others need to experience and hear it. Do not let others tell you that there is no place for marketing strategies in the church. Nothing could be further from the truth. There are storytellers, designers, videographers, photographers, directors, writers, and even marketers sitting in the pews of your church. These individuals have God-given gifts, and He wants to use them for His kingdom. Empower these individuals by allowing them to use their gifts to market the greatest message yet to be told.

# *Think It Through*

1. What is the purpose of the church?

2. Should the church invest in marketing strategies (e.g., advertising, technology (live streaming), web sites, Facebook, and email campaigns)?

# *Prayer*

Father, thank You for the gift of communication, marketing, and proclaiming! Sometimes when I sit down at my computer and work on a project, document, or even an email, I am amazed at technology. I realize I just gave away my age, but You know me now and You knew me before I was in my mother's womb. Technology scares me sometimes, just as much as the thought and idea of marketing. I guess I am thankful I do not have to have expertise in everything. All You ask from me is to have an open heart and mind to learn from others. So when it comes to the marketing strategies that our organization uses or will use, please let it be used as a tool that helps us communicate and reach those who need encouragement, hope, and help.

# *chapter twenty-eight*

## Dynamics of a Strong and Supportive Board

Look around the boardroom. Who are the leaders sitting around the table? I hope the answer was everyone! Some may have not realized that they are leaders. They may have spiritual or business aptitude and may even possess some theological insight. But when it comes to knowing how to lead the church, this might be where we see the deer in the headlight response. No one has ever taken the time to train these leaders in leading the church. This is why they were nominated, elected, and selected—to give and provide leadership to the church.

## BIBLICAL QUALIFICATIONS (1 TIMOTHY 3 AND TITUS 1)

Leaders are held to a high standard when it comes to leading themselves, their families, and the church. The first thing we are looking for is a leader who is committed to Jesus Christ. Does this leader reflect

Christ in and through his character and conduct? Does this leader reflect someone who spends time studying and applying God's Word to their lives? Does this leader reflect someone who is spiritually mature or at least growing in their faith and relationship with Christ and others? Does this leader see and serve with eyes wide open and see the big picture? Do they have a concern for the whole flock or are they focused on just self-interests or certain ministries within the church? Does the leader show compassion for the hurting and lost people who do not know Jesus? Does the leader see his board service as a calling from God or man?

For those who are about leadership development, here is an opportunity to invest in potential leaders. We have to be more intentional in identifying potential leaders and investing in them relationally (just as Jesus did with the twelve) and develop new leaders. As we invest, we move away from filling chairs and positions to filling them with passionate and focused leaders who have been equipped and trained to help fulfill the mission of the church.

## GROUP DYNAMICS

You are not a Lone Ranger in your board service. You are part of a team. There are a certain number of board members who are serving as a result of a policy that has been voted and approved by the previous or current board. Too large of a board, and communication can become a problem. Quiet board members become quieter, boisterous members become more vocal, and the lines of communication stop flowing. To enhance the team environment, leaders must take the time to create opportunities for the board to spend time together and engage in conversations outside the boardroom to get to know one another and understand one another. Wise is the board leader who creates shared experiences for board members. A board retreat helps contribute to opportunities to strengthen relationships among board members and in team building.

Building a team means that the board must work together. If a board member works better alone, board service may not be the right fit for this individual. Being a team member means there is a shared vision, everyone has a role, and there is constructive engagement. The results of an effective team reflect a team that trusts and listens to one another. Being part of a team does not mean that there will never be a disagreement or an impasse in decisions being made. What needs to be the focus is the board fulfilling its mission, seeking out the truth, challenging one another, and learning to disagree respectfully. In addition, taking the time to build emotional intelligence is critical, being aware of and regulating the emotions of individual members, the whole group, and other group members with whom they interact inside the boardroom and beyond.

## PHILOSOPHY OF MINISTRY

Do you know why your church exists? Do you know the importance of the pastor(s) in your congregation? Pastors have responded to a call from God to feed, lead, tend, and guard the flock. Of these responsibilities, leading the flock is one on which the pastor and board work closely together. The pastor's role in leading includes giving spiritual insight and guidance, discipling, and encouraging believers toward biblical and godly living. The board's role in leading requires the board to walk along beside the pastor(s) and set direction and respond to challenges and opportunities facing the church. The board at times will find itself helping guide fellow members in making wise and biblical decisions.

In saying all of this, it leads us back to the opening question: do you why the church exists? The church is God's idea. He established the church. The church is the body of Christ (Ephesians 4:1–3). The church reflects Christ and represents Him to the world. The church has been given the task to teach, preach, and fellowship (Acts 2:42). The church has been given the mandate to go into all the world (Matthew 28:19–20). What a glorious calling and responsibility.

I can see you at this point thinking, *Great stuff here, Jerry, but what does this have to do with my role as a board member?* As a board member, you need to make sure the pastors are encouraged and equipped to fulfill their calling. As a board member, you need to make sure that the budget reflects line items for Christian education of all ages, discipleship ministries, and yes, even opportunities for fellowship. As a board member, you need to make sure you are engaged in the teaching, discipling, and fellowship ministry of the church.

God has a plan for your church, and He wants to use you and involve you to reach the people in the community and around the world through the ministries of your church. How exciting for you, the church, and the pastor when God's plan is fulfilled and the mission is met because people are willing and responding with a resounding yes to be used by God. As a matter of fact, the number one job a board member has is to provide spiritual support to the pastor, ministry leaders, and the church as a whole. I do not know about you, but as a ministry leader, I would rather have a board that is spending time praying for me and the success of my ministry instead of meddling, debating, and squabbling over what is and is not getting done in the ministry.

## CHURCH GROWTH

One cannot assume that board members know or understand the dynamics of what or why pastors or ministry leaders are so passionate about church growth. Pastors get excited about when someone becomes a follower of Christ or gets baptized. If the truth be told, pastors probably should not be the only ones who get excited about these things. Every believer should share in that excitement, as this is the call of the church; this is the church being the church, and doing what the church does best. Pastors get excited about visitors! A visitor means the potential of someone becoming a regular attendee or member of the church, and in turn, they invite a friend, family member, coworker, and neighbor, and the church experiences growth. The pastor not only sees this as numerical growth, but he sees it as the potential of a new convert or someone being discipled. Again, the church is being the church and doing what the church does best.

When the church embraces the Great Commission (Matthew 28:19–20), it is engaged in a church growth strategy. Church growth does not happen by accident; it requires a vision, thought, and a strategy. A healthy church is a growing church.

What is keeping the church from experiencing growth? Is it because leadership has gotten comfortable with the way things are and has either been afraid to implement needed changes or is comfortable with the status quo? To keep the church moving forward, leaders need to have a vision and mission and develop a strategic plan. The leaders need to know where the church is going. Some have advocated forgetting the past or the glory years of the church. Allowing members to celebrate the past and look forward to the future (because the leaders have a vision for the future) gives excitement to those who have journeyed with the church as it has matured, developed, and grown.

In retail services, there is a saying: "The customer is always right." If we can take that same principle and apply it to the services we provide to first-time visitors and regular attendees, we just might see church growth as a result. As leaders, we need to ensure that the atmosphere and the worship experience itself are comfortable, inviting, and positive. Church members want to be part of a church that cares for them and gives them opportunities to serve and where there is evidence of proper management of church resources (good stewardship).

Church growth matters because there are still lost souls that need to know and experience the love, forgiveness, and hope of salvation that only Jesus can give. The last time I drove to church or took a walk in my neighborhood, or even logged into my neighborhood watch app, it was apparent that there are people still choosing not to be followers of Jesus Christ or connected with a local church. I still have friends and neighbors who need Jesus. Concentrating on the needs of those outside the church helps keep the focus on outreach and evangelism to grow the church.

Here are questions for your consideration: Why are you serving as a board member? Has the church reached and completed its mission? Are there still children, youth, young adults, middle-aged adults, and senior adults who need to hear and know the life-changing message of the gospel? Can you make sure as a board member that your church, staff, and fellow board members keep talking about the importance of church growth?

# Pause and Reflect

Take a moment to reflect on what scripture has to say about serving as a board member. Space has been created for you to write your responses to the questions asked in this section.

## Thanksgiving and Prayer

> I have not stopped giving thanks for you, remembering you in my prayers. I keep asking that the God of our Lord Jesus Christ, the glorious Father, may give you the Spirit of wisdom and revelation, so that you may know him better. I pray that the eyes of your heart may be enlightened in order that you may know the hope to which he has called you, the riches of his glorious inheritance in his holy people, and his incomparably great power for us who believe. That power is the same as the mighty strength.
> —Ephesians 1:16–19 (NIV)

Who do you give God thanks for in your life? Is it a parent, spouse, grandparent, pastor, teacher, or friend? Hopefully, there is someone who has influenced or impacted your life in a positive kind of way. We all need a Paul in our life, and we all need to be a Paul to someone else. What I mean by this is I need to make sure I am praying for someone and I need someone to pray for me. I know I can either call or text them and know they will intercede in prayer on my behalf. I need someone who will be honest, open, and trustworthy. Someone who is not afraid to tell or show me where I may have missed the mark or could have done better. This "Paul" is not pointing out my flaws, mistakes, or even sins in judgment but wants to help me mature and grow in my faith. These people simply are being a Paul in my life.

What would happen if we created communities of faith where it was the norm to hear people praying for and encouraging one another? What would happen if the fellowship of the church became so contagious with laughter and joy that people from the outside did not want to miss out on the experience of whatever these Christians are experiencing with one another? Make it a point to pray for your fellow board members. They are not your enemies; they are your fellow brothers and sisters in Christ. Let us become Pauls to one another!

# *Think It Through*

1. Is there a culture of appreciation expressed or encouraged within the boardroom or from fellow board members?

2. Does the board work collaboratively? If yes, what factors contribute to this type of relationship? If not, what can be done as a board to change this dynamic?

3. Are the goals being accomplished through the work of the board? If not, why not?

4. Is the board passionate about making the church or organization the best it can be?

# *Prayer*

Father, thank You for the church. We realize the church is Your idea. You established it and have called it to help accomplish Your will. You have called men and women to lead and guide the church. You have called people to preach the Word, equip the saints, and minister to a hurting world. The church has not always gotten it right. You have always been there to guide us, lead us, and show us the way to go. May we be people who lean into and obey, listen, and follow Your voice as we lead the church, Your church.

# chapter twenty-nine

## Ineffective or Effective Boards

There are both positive and negative ways to view life, work, church, family, friends, government, and yes, even the church. Evaluating, being curious, asking questions, and seeking clarification are all traits that speak to board members being effective board members. Sadly though, many board members fail to be engaged, struggle with asking questions, and are only interested in doing the minimum in their board service. Oftentimes, leaders have created a culture whereby questions from board members are not welcome and the standard of operations has become "We will explain to you what you need to know." This mode of operation only contributes to board members who are not engaged or complacent, do not add value, and fail to fulfill their fiduciary duties. Their board service becomes routine, and board meetings can become scripted and nonparticipatory for members.

Ineffective boards can keep the organization from achieving its goals by being uncooperative with other board members. Indecisive behavior can contribute to ineffective board behavior. Coming to board meetings unprepared and not taking the time to review or read reports ahead of time can contribute to being an ineffective board member. Lack of motivation is also a contributing factor to ineffective board service. It is the responsibility of the board to be engaged in an annual assessment of their individual behavior and contribution to the board and the organization as a whole. The board governs itself. An effective board is more likely to assess themselves before an ineffective board.

Another factor effective boards consider is term limits. The bylaws of the organization should address term limits. Stroman (2017) recommends to "include a provision in your bylaws limiting the number of years board members can serve." Keep in mind there are best practices when it comes to board governance and monitoring and maintaining decorum in the boardroom. Bylaws have their purpose and are very important for an organization. Bylaws can be amended, if necessary, in the best interests of the organization. Any changes or amendments made to the bylaws need to be recorded in the minutes exactly why the temporary bylaws were changed or suspended, the action that was taken and voted on. There should be a time limit put on the amendment, and the minutes will reflect the individual who is affected by this change and why.

Board size has to be a factor to consider in addressing effective boards as well. This is one of those proverbial questions that gets asked a lot in board webinars, seminars, and workshops. How many board members should our board have? Stroman (2017) states,

> There isn't just one correct answer. Each organization should have the number of board members that is right for that particular entity, at that precise time in its development, to sufficiently serve the needs of the board.

Now that we have settled the recommended board size, we have to explore the topic of term limits. The first place a board would look for the answer to this question is in the bylaws of the organization, that the board has taken the time to review, approve, and reference as needed. This is one of those questions that cannot be answered the same for every church and organization.

It is easy for boards to dismiss or show disinterest in the term limit process as review might lead to the discovery of necessary revisions, and revisions mean amending the bylaws, and amendments mean delving into details, and details have not always been the strong suit of too many boards.

Let's discuss term limits and the benefits of term limits.

- It develops leaders.
- It allows for diversification of the board by allowing new members into the decision-making process.
- Previous members can become advocates for the organization as they step into new roles within the group.
- It allows response to rapidly changing needs.
- It prevents authority from resting within a small circle of individuals.

Of course, rotating board members may result in some loss of institutional memory. However, nothing precludes these members from rejoining the board after taking some time off.

Boards that take the time to review the bylaws every year, or at least every five years, reflect care and concern about being aligned with the best governance practices. Best governance practices lend themselves to a board that is open, honest, and transparent.

Earlier in the book, I mentioned that *Robert's Rules of Order* was not a form of governance. If the truth is to be told, this caught some of you by surprise! *Robert's Rules of Order* is widely known as parliamentary procedure, ensuring that meetings are fair, efficient, democratic, and orderly (https://www.umcnic.org/media/files/annual%20conference/RobertsRulesCheatSheet.pdf). Basic parliamentary procedures should be part of the board member orientation. The goal for board members is to be engaged and participate in efficient and productive board meetings.

Being a board member who is curious and is allowed to ask questions, seek clarification, and is observant of what is going on both inside and outside the organization is being a board member who will add value and informed perspectives to the discussions, decisions being made, and the overall mission.

Effective boards ensure an amicable board/staff relationship exists by clearly defining the roles and responsibilities of the board and staff. In my particular denomination, it is clearly a known fact that the staff does not report to the board. The staff is hired by the senior pastor and the only involvement the board has in the hiring process is the budget is approved for staff position recommendations. The staff reports to the senior pastor and attends board meetings at the invitation of the senior pastor and submits monthly ministry reports to the board at the request of the senior pastor for the purpose of accountability and ministry effectiveness. In addition, the board members know and understand their own roles and responsibilities. Board members contribute to the success of the organization when they clearly understand and operate with an understanding of their respective roles and responsibilities. The board chair contributes to the effectiveness of the board by fulfilling his role with a high degree of professionalism and exemplifying leadership characteristics that complement and encourage both staff and board efforts.

Effective board members who walk in alignment with spiritual and practical best practices are able to best serve the pastor and the church. And most importantly, these wonderful partners in ministry fulfill all God wants to do in their lives and that of the church.

# Pause and Reflect

Take a moment to reflect on what scripture has to say about serving as a board member. Space has been created for you to write your responses to the questions asked in this section.

## Whatever You Do

> Whatever you do, work at it with all your heart, as working for the Lord, not for human masters, since you know that you will receive an inheritance from the Lord as a reward. It is the Lord Christ you are serving.
> —Colossians 3:23–24 (NIV)

Paul is reminding the believers in Colossae not to work and live in such a way that resembles getting by or doing the bare minimum in our service. Through our work, we are reflecting and serving Christ. From the lowest to the executive, from the volunteer to the paid staff, from the committee members to board members, we are all serving Christ and should do and give our best for Him. As we do our work for the Lord, we experience spiritual growth. Is it not amazing that God knew as we use our gifts for Him that we would grow and mature in our faith—and ultimately He receives the glory out of our work?

Let us be people who offer through our service to the church that is effective, efficient, productive, and pleasing to God. No more ineffective work or service. Let us keep moving the needle, organization, church, and ourselves forward as we do our work for the Lord.

# *Think It Through*

1. Does the board possess the required competencies to fulfill its duties?

2. Does the board possess the ideal mix of competencies to handle the most pressing issue on the agenda?

3. Does the board engage in an annual self-evaluation by asking the following questions of themselves:

   - Do I attend board meetings regularly?
   - Do the advance meeting materials provide sufficient information to prepare for meetings? Are they clear and well organized, and do they highlight the most critical issues for consideration?
   - Do I come to board meetings prepared, having thoroughly studied all premeeting materials?
   - Can the board clearly articulate and communicate the organization's strategic plan?

# Prayer

Father, as I read the words *effective* and *ineffective,* they cause me to stop and reflect on my service not only as a board member but as an individual living in a mixed-up world. It causes me to stop and think about the other areas of my life. Am I being effective or ineffective in my day-to-day life? In my work life? In my family life? In all that I do, how would You evaluate me? My prayer is that You would find me an effective servant. Living a life that is pleasing to You. Living a life where I can hear You say, "Well done, good and faithful servant."

# chapter thirty

## Expectations

We made it to day thirty! It has been a journey. Who would have ever thought that there was so much to being a board member? The information included in this book was not to overwhelm, discourage, or cause you to respond, "Thank you for the opportunity, but no thank you." The purpose was to inform, educate, and let you know there are expectations in serving as a board member. Expectations? No one likes hearing that word or even living it out! But we all have expectations. Think about the world in which you live or find yourself living in. I expect my coffee to be fresh and hot when I order it and pick it up at my local drive-thru. Does it always meet my expectations? Nope! I expect my local grocery store to always have the staples I need on the shelf, fully stocked, and right where it was the last time I went shopping for that particular item. Does it always meet my expectations? Nope! I expect the local politicians to always vote the way I think they should vote. Do they always meet my expectations? Nope! I expect board members to always make the right decisions, carry out their fiduciary duties, and leap from tall buildings and have more power than a locomotive! Have they always met my expectations? Nope! So is it acceptable to have expectations of board members? A simple answer is yes.

Expectations help board members to realize that their service is needed and has meaning and purpose. If you have board members who are not engaged and seem to cause more frustration than being of help to the leaders of the organization, it might be time to evaluate the expectations. It is important for organizational leaders to remember that board members are volunteers with time commitments and external pressures.

Expectations can be clarified at the onboarding of new board members or at the board orientation. Some boards have moved to a strategy of managing themselves by implementing a nominating committee. The purpose of this committee is to ensure that the best possible people are identified as potential board members. Board member orientation and training have been relegated to the governance or board development committee.

When a church or organization experiences unexpressed or unidentified expectations, it can contribute to a failure of relationships and organizational success. As a board member, you want to know that your service is making a positive difference. This means that leaders of the organization need to communicate and clarify the needs of the organization and ask for your involvement and address expectations from both you and the leaders. If you want to build high levels of trust with your leaders and board, have specific outcomes in mind and make sure you communicate them. Do not expect people to have telepathic powers. You should not expect people to understand intuitively what you want. Explaining the background and circumstances behind decisions is crucial for the organization to understand complex board decisions.

As stated at the beginning of this work, I have seen the good, bad, and ugly when it comes to boards. As we have read over these thirty chapters, the work of the board can be tiring and time-consuming, but it is worth the effort as individuals are given an opportunity to serve, share their skills and expertise, and perhaps even grow in their knowledge of what it truly means to be board members.

A few months ago, I had a passing conversation with a colleague in the airport on my way to a conference to present a board governance workshop to a group of pastors. When the colleague inquired about my topic and I shared what I was going to present, he rolled his eyes and responded with a chuckle and statement along the lines of this: "Well, everyone knows that the topic needs to be addressed, but no one really wants to fix the problem." I walked away from that conversation while shaking my head and thinking, *You really did not hear or care to hear that I was going to encourage a group of pastors to address and give them some solutions and help to what has proven to be a problem and continues to be a problem, not only for pastors but many churches.*

Benjamin Franklin said it best. "If you fail to plan, you are planning to fail." I do not know about you, but I want to change the board culture and behavior that seems to have been passed down through what I have defined as "generational board behavior." This simply means I watched my father, uncle, brother, mother, grandmother, aunt, and cousin all serve as board members, and I guess they survived the ordeal. If they can do it, I can do it. I do not know what I am doing, but I will just watch those who have been serving year after year and learn from them.

It is time we change the boardroom culture and behavior. It is time we train, equip, and encourage board members to serve as an act of worship—worship (and board service) that is pleasing to our Lord and Savior.

# Pause and Reflect

Take a moment to reflect on what scripture has to say about serving as a board member. Space has been created for you to write your responses to the questions asked in this section.

## The Parable of the Bags of Gold

> Again, it will be like a man going on a journey, who called his servants and entrusted his wealth to them. To one he gave five bags of gold, to another two bags, and to another one bag,[a] each according to his ability. Then he went on his journey.
> —Matthew 25:14–15 (NIV)

God gives each of us responsibility, and that responsibility is always accompanied by expectations. Every one of us is accountable to God for our performance and behavior.

We have potential, power, and resources at our disposal. These are not for our own good but for the good of the kingdom of God. What would God's response be to how you are using these? Would He find you faithful? Would He respond, "Well done, good and faithful servant," or "You wicked, lazy servant"?

Here's a takeaway from this parable that I find refreshing. It is kind of odd to think there is a glimmer of hope found there, is it not? When we first read this parable and compare what the three servants did with their master's money, we get a glimpse of the who, what, why, and how. The first two double their master's money. The third saw his master as "one who was a hard man, harvesting where he had not sown and gathering where he did not plant seeds." His view of his master was not very high. I wonder if this parable is not teaching us to take a look at our view of God. And does our view of God keep us from serving Him unconditionally? Does our view of God set us up for expectations of God that He will never be pleased with us? He does not love, accept, care, or trust us?

Here is the good news you can take away from this parable: God does love you. God does trust you. Discover in your board service how God can use you to invest and build His kingdom. Maybe the question is this: how am I doing with managing what God has given to me?

# Think It Through

1. Does your church have expectations for its board members?

2. Are those expectations written down?

3. Does each board member know and understand what is expected of him?

4. Do they agree with those expectations? How do you know?

# Prayer

Father, as I read this parable, I have to be honest. It is challenging. In this parable, we get a glimpse of who You are and how You view Your servants. You believe in us and You entrust us with so much. Give us the wisdom to know how to be good stewards of those resources. To be good stewards of our time, talents, and treasures. Give us wisdom and help us realize that You are God who loves us unconditionally. Help us to love others in the same way.

# *works cited*

Church of the Nazarene. *Manual,* 2017–2021.

Church of the Nazarene. *Nazarene Safe,* 2022.

Colorado District Church of the Nazarene. *Colorado District Church of the Nazarene Pastoral Review,* 2022.

Diehl, James, general superintendent emeritus, Church of the Nazarene. Review/Comments/Thoughts-Jerry W. Storz, March 11, 2022.

Fram, Eugene. "Why Are Some Nonprofit Boards Missing the Mark? What to Do?" *Nonprofit Management,* WordPress, June 12, 2022, non-profit-management-dr-fram.com/2022/06/12/why-are-some-nonprofit-boards-missing-the-mark-what-to-do-4/. Accessed June 12, 2022.

King, Thomas J., and Daniel G. Powers. "A Student's Guide to Exegetical Work." Nazarene Bible College, 2021, 1–50.

Storz, Jerry W. "The Five Functions." *Entre Ninos,* no. 28, June 2020, 1–53.

Stroman, M. Kent. *The Intentional Board.* CharityChannel Press, 2017.

# *appendix a*

## Different Governance Structures

Community Literacy of Ontario
Cindy Davidson
June 2014
www.communityLiteracyofontario.ca

Governance structures can be put into two basic categories: policy boards and administrative boards. Policy governing boards develop policy and hire an Executive Director to implement the policy whereas administrative governing boards play a more hands-on role in managing the organization with the support of committees and staff. Within these two broad categories of governance, there are four common types of board models:

1. **Policy Board**: Sometimes referred to as Management-Team Board, this model is commonly used in non-profit organizations. Several committees help carry out the activities of the organization, and the relationship between the board and staff is one of a partnership.
2. **Policy Governance Board**: Sometimes referred to as a 'Carver Board' after founder John Carver, this model has a more formal structure. The board operates as a whole, using one voice and rarely works with committees. The Executive Director is given a very clear scope and role as well as limits about what she/ he can undertake, and the main emphasis of the board is on

policy development. For a more complete definition of the Policy Governance Board Model, visit www.carvergovernance.com/model.htm.

3. **Working Board**: Directors on this type of board play a more hands-on role with some of the administrative functions of the organization such as public relations, financial management, program planning and personnel. It's not uncommon for these boards to not have any staff.

4. **Collective Board**: Sometimes known as a cooperative or coalition, a Collective Board also carries out many administrative functions of the organization. These boards are comprised of like-minded people that support a specific goal. Staff and directors operate together as a single entity. There is not usually an Executive Director, and often there is no voting as everyone works within a consensus model.

# *appendix b*

## Professional Standard of Conduct/Code of Conduct
## (CRC Code of Conduct for Ministry Leaders)
### crcna.org

### PREAMBLE

In Philippians 2 the apostle Paul brings to his Philippian readers the words of a hymn in which Christ Jesus is acknowledged as being, in his very nature, God. Among other things, this means that Christ is the one to whom all power belongs.

The hymn goes on to say that Christ did not consider equality with God as something to be used to his own advantage. In fact, he made himself nothing, taking the very nature of a servant, and humbling himself toward a life-sacrificing kind of obedience. In other words, he used his power for the thriving of others.

All of us who are united to Christ by faith and who serve in the life of the church are called, in this passage and others, to this way of being. Jesus himself, in response to the desire for power expressed by his disciples, called them (and us) to use power to serve people, a way of holding power that confronts and contrasts with the ways that the world uses power.[1]

Not only do we have this call from Christ, but we actually have Jesus

---

[1] See Mark 10:35–45. Note that there are other scripture texts that address the use of power to bless, such as 1 Peter 5:1–4. In addition, there are texts that describe abuses of power and the damage that such abuses cause (see, for example, 2 Samuel 11 and Ezekiel 34).

living and growing within us (Gal. 2:20). As a result, we find ourselves being transformed into the kind of people who hold and use power in a Christlike way.

That being said, until Christ returns and brings us to perfection, we will continue to wrestle with the urge to misuse power and abuse others. Ugly realities such as verbal, emotional, psychological, physical, sexual, and spiritual abuse are found among us. The power that we hold by virtue of our person or our position can always be twisted into the project of building our own kingdoms at the expense of others. This is true for pastors, lay ministry leaders, and church members alike.

In awareness of these ugly realities and in the beautiful hope of Christ's transforming work, the following code of conduct is offered for ministry leaders. It is shaped by Scripture and by commitments found in our confessional statements and contemporary testimonies.[2] It emerges out of a response by Synod 2018 to patterns of abuse that had been brought to its attention[3] and is aimed at preventing such abuse in the future. May God's peace be among us.

---

[2] See *Belgic Confession,* Article 28, and *Heidelberg Catechism,* Q. and A., 55, 107, 111. See also the statement in the Confession of Belhar that says, "We believe … that the church as the possession of God must stand where the Lord stands, namely against injustice and with the wronged; that in following Christ the church must witness against all the powerful and privileged who selfishly seek their own interests and thus control and harm others" (Confession of Belhar, Article 4). Further, in *Our World Belongs to God,* we read that the church is a "new community," gathered by God, in which "all are welcome"; that the church's mission in this broken world is a mission of proclaiming the gospel and its implications for life today; and that "restored in Christ's presence, shaped by his life, this new community lives out the ongoing story of God's reconciling love, announces the new creation, and works for a world of justice and peace." Such statements describe the mission of the church in general and provide foundation for the specific code of conduct presented here.

[3] Bev Sterk's overture to Synod 2018, titled "Address Patterns of Abuse of Power That Violate the Sacred Trust Given to Leaders and Recognize How These Hinder Due Process and Healing," and appendices specifically related to it, can be found in the *Agenda for Synod 2018,* pp. 282–307 (see crcna.org/Synod Resources). The subsequent action of Synod 2018 was to form an Abuse of Power Committee to study "how the CRCNA can best address patterns of abuse of power at all levels of the denomination" (*Acts of Synod 2018,* pp. 523–24). The work of Synod 2019

# CODE OF CONDUCT

Abuse of power is a misuse of position, authority, or influence to take advantage of, manipulate, or control. Abuse of power occurs when a person with power, regardless of its source, uses that power to harm and/or influence another for personal gain at the other's expense. All abuse by faith leaders within the church is also spiritual abuse and has spiritual impacts that often heighten the harm caused to individuals and to the family of God. (For more background, see *Acts of Synod 2019*, pp. 587–615).

As a ministry leader, I commit to the following:

## Confidentiality

I will use confidentiality appropriately, which means I will hold in confidence whatever information is not mine to share.

I will not use information shared with me in confidence in order to elevate my position or to depreciate that of others.

My use of confidentiality will also be guided by mandatory reporting as required by law.

## Relational

I will speak and act, in all my personal and professional relations, in ways that follow the pattern of Christ, who used his power to serve (1 Pet. 5; Mark 10; Phil. 2; 2 Tim. 4:2).

I will conduct myself with respect, love, integrity, and truthfulness toward all—regardless of position, status, race, gender, age, or ability.

To the best of my ability, I will contribute to an environment of hospitality.

---

related to this overture can be found in the *Acts of Synod 2019*, pp. 794–96 (see crcna.org/Synod Resources). The particular recommendation calling for a code of conduct is recommendation 3 (p. 795).

*Financial*

I will ensure that funds are used for their intended ministry purposes.

In all financial matters, including the acceptance of gifts, I will act with scrupulous honesty, transparency, and appropriate accountability.

I will appropriately use accepted accounting practices and regular reviews and/or audits.

*Intimate Relationships*

I will maintain standards and appropriate boundaries in all relationships, which are informed by the Scriptures.

I will keep all of my professional relationships free from inappropriate emotional and sexual behaviors. This includes not engaging in inappropriate intimate contact or a sexual relationship, unwanted physical contact, sexual comments, gestures, or jokes.

*Safety*

I will actively promote a safe environment where all persons are respected and valued, where any form of abuse, bullying, or harassment is neither tolerated nor allowed to take place.

I will report known or suspected cases of physical, sexual, or emotional abuse or neglect of minors to the proper government authorities.

I will support adults who disclose physical, sexual, or emotional abuse in a way that appropriately empowers the person who has been victimized.

*Spiritual*

I will acknowledge the use of Scripture and the Spirit's work in the community of the church and, therefore, refrain from presuming to be the sole "voice of God."

I will use my position as a way to serve the body of believers, rather than myself, for the common good and the cultivation of the gifts of the Spirit.

*Additional Commitments*

I will work within my professional competence, especially in counseling situations, and I will refer individuals to other professionals as appropriate.

I will promote truthfulness, transparency, and honesty in all of my work.

I will disclose any perceived or actual conflict of interest.

In all that I do, I will seek to use my position, power, and authority prudently and humbly, and in nonexploitive ways.

In the event that I misuse my power, either intentionally or unintentionally, as a ministry leader, I will acknowledge the harm that has been caused and the trust that has been broken, and I will actively seek restoration with justice, compassion, truth, and grace. I will humbly submit to the insight and accountability of others to ensure that I use any power entrusted to me fully in service to Christ.

Printed in the United States
by Baker & Taylor Publisher Services